DAILY MESSAGES
FROM MY WINDOW

DAILY MESSAGES

From My Window

By Dr. Jossie E. Owens

© 2019 by Dr. Jossie E. Owens

All rights reserved. This book or any portion thereof may not be reproduced or used in any manner whatsoever without the express written permission of the publisher except for the use of brief quotations in a book review. All quotations of scripture in this book are taken from the Holy Bible, the New International Version.

ISBN: 9781705827376

DEDICATION

This book is dedicated to my mom, Mamie Kelley White. She was the best mother in the whole wide world, and she taught me so much about God and life looking out the window of our third-floor apartment. She left this world far too soon in life.

JANUARY 1

~Day 1~

Get Rid of It

I am excited about journeying with you through these messages from my Daily Window this year. Let's walk in faith, believing that God can change us, mold us, instruct us, and teach us to have a stronger and deeper walk with *Him*. Let's walk the path of getting rid of the extra junk. I was in my pantry the other day, and as I picked up a can of tomato paste, I noticed that the date on the can had expired. The product was not as fresh as it should have been. I got rid of the can. I started to check the dates on other products in the closet and remove them from the shelves. Today is the first day of a brand-new year. We need to check ourselves and take stock. We need to get rid of stuff that has truly expired within our souls. We need to get rid of any old memories or disappointments that have been keeping us from our full potential. We need to check our labels today and take stock of ourselves. We need to get rid of negative vibes and make room for positive new beginnings.

JANUARY 2

~Day 2~

Pause Button

Good morning. This is the second day of a brand-new year, and we want to get it right. We want to stay on the right path that we committed to for this year. Remember, we want to continue to be thankful to God for allowing us to cross over into another new year. Praise God. Always remember to praise God first. If we praise God first, we will definitely get into less trouble. Trust me. I know from the window where I sit.

Secondly, we want to hit our mental "pause button" on the negative thoughts we may process today. We will not carry these negative thoughts with us. We choose to walk in freedom from all chains today. Our chains are gone, and we have been set free. We will not allow our minds to close off our freedom of joy, peace, love, or grace of mind. If you find yourself slipping into some negative thinking today, hit your mental pause button. Say to yourself, "We are not going there today. No way. We have been set free from these negative things, and we will walk in the joy of the spirit of God."

Walk today in the newness of your committed life with Jesus Christ. Please don't allow yourself to walk in fear. Remember, you have a pause button.

JANUARY 3

~Day 3~

Progressive Start

When I first looked out my window this morning, the sky was cloudy and dark. It was okay by me. I was having a progressive start to my day. Do you know what a progressive start to your day means? It is when you start your day by your own inner clock. You wake up not to an alarm set or by having a scheduled meeting of activities in your mind. You start your day by your own personal choice. You take your time in everything that you do when you have a progressive start. Do you know how mentally freeing this type of day can be? Not to have to be someplace at an appointed time or having to fulfill some established commitment? You have freedom to be creative in your thoughts; some of my best ideas have come from having a progressive wake-up day. This is the third day of a new year; think about slowing down your pace, and plan for a progressive start to your day. You will be a healthier person in mind, soul, and body.

JANUARY 4

~Day 4~

Your Street

As I look out my window this morning, I look up and down the street. I have just finished my morning devotions, and I am thankful to God. I am thankful for the gifts of sight, smell, taste, hearing, and touch. I am thankful for sight. I do not take my sight for granted anymore. I use to just assume I would always have perfect sight. Did you? I can see automobiles traveling and passing by my window. I see people walking their dogs before they have to leave for work. As I look out at the street, I see beautiful, tall trees that could tell their own stories. We should not take our senses for granted because there is nothing in this world that is guaranteed. The only sure thing that we truly have in this life is the love of Jesus Christ.

    I am thankful for God reminding me today to remember the unexpected blessings that He has given each of us. As you look out your window or walk down your street today, remember to thank God for all the blessings that He has given you. Walk under His anointing today and every day.

JANUARY 5

~Day 5~

Rainy Day

As I woke up this morning, I heard a tapping sound on my windowpane. I heard the sounds of rain. I have to be honest with you, I love the sound of rain tapping on my roof. I feel safe and warm inside my soul. Rain seems to speak to my soul and has a calming effect on my spirit. What about you? On rainy days I seem to process things in a more thoughtful way. Do you? Rain can have a great influence on the body and spirit. Enjoy some of the rainstorms in your life. You might be surprised that rain can cause your day to be more positive in nature. Listen to the sound of living nature, and enjoy the communication of living life. Enjoy the spirit and nature of the gift that God has given us this day. Be calm. Be focused. Experience and find joy in every day.

JANUARY 6

~Day 6~

The Sixth Day

This is the sixth day of the new year. Are you still rejoicing that you were allowed to cross over into a new year? I pray so. You know things grow old pretty fast for us humans. I was in the gym yesterday and could not get on a treadmill. Why? Everyone has resolved to lose a few pounds. This is a great thing, but will the treadmills still be full by the end of January? I pray so. Everything is new and fresh on January 1. We made all of kinds of commitments to do better and to be better at the beginning of the year. We can be physically and spiritually better if we do things in the right order and pace. What I notice at the gym is that new members come and take every class that is offered. They have not been in the gym for years, and all of a sudden, they are taking fifty classes. They will eventually get tired or hurt and say the gym is not for them. We are not going to be one of those folks this year. Are we?

    We have committed to do better and to be better in all phases of our lives by taking one step at a time. The most important relationship that we can cultivate this day and every day is our relationship with Jesus Christ. If we cultivate this relationship daily, then all other relationships will be better. This is the sixth day of the new year. Remember, that this is a new day and a new opportunity to know our Lord.

JANUARY 7

~Day 7~

Check-On Person

Are you the "check-on person" in your family or friend circle? Do you even know what a check-on person is? It is the one person in the group circle who checks to make sure that everyone is okay. Are you that person in your family or group? I am the check-on person within my circle. I call my siblings and friends daily to make sure that they are alive and well. I call them and send little note cards of encouragement. It is important to have a check-on person. This person is the one who continually ties the unit together. We all need a check-on person in our lives. I have a friend who is also the check-on person in her circle of family and friends. We both decided that we don't take it personally that other folks don't call us first. Take a few minutes out of your day, and give someone in your group a call or a note of encouragement. Don't live in your mind with the cardinal rules that say, "Someone has to call me first" or "I made the last call; they have to call me back." Don't keep a scorecard. Trust me, those scorecards are not your friends. Enjoy your day. Make some positive check-ins today. Become a *check-on person*.

JANUARY 8

~Day 8~

Maintain a Five Day

Good morning. Let me share some wisdom from my windowsill; you will not always be going to be at a ten in life. Every day is not going to be a ten day. Every day was not meant to be a ten day. If you find yourself at some point of having a five day, that's okay. Trust me, you are staying the course of life. I don't believe that Jesus was always at a ten either. We read about some of His mountaintop experiences, and He did not have those times every day. What I love about Jesus is that He dealt with everyday issues just like you and me. He had to deal with family, church, government, and people issues all the time. I believe He had a number of five days, and He made it through.

We will make it through today, and tomorrow, and the day after that. If you were to rate yourself today, on a scale of one to ten, with ten being on the mountaintop, you find yourself at a five. Good. Five is good. Five is staying the course. Just being a five and maintaining life today is good. Trust me. I know from where I look out from my windowsill.

JANUARY 9

~Day 9~

Special Day

Did you know that today is a special day? Well, it is truly a special day. One of the definitions of special is "having a specific purpose." Did you know that you have a specific purpose today? Well, you do. This is a special day because you have been allowed to be a part of this great day. I don't know what the day holds for you, but I know that because you are a part of it, it is indeed special. You were created by the Heavenly Father, and He created a special person in you. He has a specific purpose for your life. Sometimes, things seem dark and lost. Sometimes, we don't know whether or not we can find our way out of a maze.

Trust me, as I look out my window, I see light ahead of your journey. I have walked some of the roads that you are walking now. The roads of doubt, pain, sorrow, hurt, darkness, and despair. I also walked and now live in the roads of joy, love, forgiveness, and peace. This is a special day. You want to know why? God is with us, and He is walking with us. He has a special day planned just for you today. Will you allow Him to walk with you today and show you your specific purpose? Today and every day. Trust Him. He will guide you and instruct you on the right path of life.

JANUARY 10

~Day 10~

Recollections

To recall memories can be good sometimes. Every January, I take a journey down memory lane. I talk with my sisters about the good old days when snow fell at the rate of three feet an hour. When snow cones were huge and we could not finish them. We talk about the size of the french fries we use to purchase for ten cents at the corner stone. The corner store had everything. You would get enough fries to feed an army for only ten cents. We share about the submarine sandwiches we use to purchase for only twenty-five cents—the best subs in the world. The sub shop just closed a few years ago. We cried. So many memories. So many recollections—good, bad, and ugly.

We recall as a family all the times that God heard our prayers and our needs. We recall how God brought us through desperate times of need. Recollections can be good sometimes and always when God is at the central of the recollections. Think about some of the recollections that have brought you to this particular day, time, and place. Remember, Christ can be at the center of whatever recollections you are making now.

JANUARY 11

~Day 11~

Coldness

It is freezing outside as I watch people all bundled up in their winter clothing. The heating system in my house is straining to keep the rooms warm. I am grateful that we purchased new windows for our home this year. I don't hear the wind blowing through the windowpanes. It may be cold outside, but I am enjoying the comforts of warm living. I have a great cup of tea and am enjoying reading from my favorite book.

Today is a new day, and we must embrace the fullness of this day. I am grateful to God for allowing each of us to experience all the joys that life has to bring our way. It may be cold outside, but you can experience the warmth of the sun in your soul today. When we have Christ at the center of everything in our existence, we are free in our souls. We don't have to carry our trials, tribulations, burdens, and struggles by ourselves. We can lean on the everlasting love and shoulders of our Heavenly Father. Maybe you are experiencing some type of coldness today. Remember, you have a God who can place sunshine in your life, even on a dark and dreary day. As you look out your window today and you say to yourself, "It's cold outside," it might be cold outside, but you can have a warm heart full of the love of Jesus Christ. Invite Him in, and you will not be cold in your soul. He is at your front door waiting.

JANUARY 12

~Day 12~

Mood

Good morning. I have a question for you today in the Daily Window. What is your mood like today? How did you wake up this morning? In what type of mood? Positive, negative, excited, fearful, inspired, or depressed? What do I mean by the word "mood?" My definition of a mood is a "distinct state of emotional feeling of the body, spirit, and mind."

The questions are "What state of mind are you allowing yourself to be in, on this beautiful cold winter day? What did you carry with you to bed last night, that continues to linger in your mind this morning? Good? Bad? Positive or negative? How will this mood or thought affect your new day?" You have a choice on how your day is going to play out in life today. Your mood can add or subtract from the opportunities of this new day. Are you still upset by the comments of yesterday? Today is a new day with new opportunities, new memories to be had and made. Every day can be a true new beginning of a new story. We choose how we will interact and engage with life and people. Start today with a new mood in Christ. Try first interacting with Jesus, and I know that your mood will shift into a higher gear.

JANUARY 13

~Day 13~

Do Not Be Afraid

It is my prayer that you have started this beautiful day living in peace and not fear. Do not be afraid of this new day. Fear robs us of the joy that we can experience in life. Too many people are afraid in this great and vast world. You want to know how I know that there are so many people who are afraid? We have too many people doing things in society that are done by acts of fear. We are not to be afraid in this life. We, who believe and live and serve the Risen King, do not have to walk in fear or apprehension. Our God will be with us in all aspects of our lives.

We are not to be afraid of the darkness of the day or the terrors of the night. Our Heavenly Father is with us.

Saying that He is with us does not mean that we will not go through periods of pain, darkness, and loss. Many people leave the faith because they thought that their Christian journey would be perfect and that they would not experience sorrow or disappointment. Jesus never said that we would have a life free of troubles. What the scriptures do say is that He will walk alongside us. He will be with us and will give us the sufficient grace to meet each challenge. Jesus will walk with us through the darkness and bring us out into the marvelous light. You will not travel alone. You have a Friend to guide your path today and every day. Do not be afraid.

JANUARY 14

~Day 14~

Continue

As we are allowed to walk on this earth, we must continue to put our trust in our Heavenly Father. As you look out the window of life this morning, raise your head to the sky and say, "I trust in you, Lord, and I will continue to walk with you daily." Continue to linger in His arms today and give Him all your trials, cares, and burdens. Did you give Him all of your struggles? His arms are more than sufficient to carry all of our burdens, problems, and concerns. Trust me, we serve a big God. Learn to continue to trust Him and not be so fearful.

JANUARY 15

~Day 15~

Comments

Good morning, my Daily Window watchers. Other people's comments can have an effect on us. However, we make a conscious mental choice on whether we will allow their words to have either a positive or negative affect on our lives. You control and direct the course of your life with God's help and guidance. Don't allow someone to say something to you today that puts your soul and spirit in a difficult place. You can potentially give that individual too much power or control within your life space on this earth. Don't allow anyone or anything toxic to enter your space today. Walk today in the anointing of the Lord God, and take control of your day! Don't allow other people's craziness to spoil the beauty of this precious day. You are loved today, and every day on this great planet that we call Earth. Embrace the day without taking in toxic comments or views. Rather, my dear Window watcher, take in love, joy, and peace.

JANUARY 16

~Day 16~

The Gift

You have a new day to learn more about yourself and the people around you. You have the gift of life today. You have an opportunity to interact with people you have never met before. We have a chance today to right some hurt or wrong has been done to us or to others. We have the gift of life today. What a gift! Each day that we are allowed to open this special gift, it has the potential of new opportunities and adventures. I don't know what happened to you yesterday or what type of emotions you expended to the world yesterday. Let it go, my friend; yesterday is gone, and you will never get it back. Today is a new day. Whatever happened yesterday is gone and is now in the past. Today, you can experience the gift of a brand-new day. What a gift! Don't waste it. Open the package, and enjoy the gift of life today.

JANUARY 17

~Day 17~

Unexpected Turns

How are you doing today? I trust that you had a great night of rest and that your soul is at peace this morning. Today is a new day and a new day of unexpected turns. Today is a new day of opportunities for unexpected joy and life-changing experiences. Don't be afraid to venture down different roads and paths today. We do not have to always walk the same road. We can journey down different life streets, as long as our Lord and Savior is doing the directing and guiding. Trust God. Do not be afraid of new unexpected turns and ventures. You may receive a call today that presents a new or unexpected challenge. Do not walk in fear or despair. We serve a mighty God, and He walks with us and talks with us daily. Trust Him to take you on that unexpected turn today and every day.

JANUARY 18

~Day 18~

Chosen

Did you know that you are chosen? You are truly special. You have been chosen to participate and engage in this truly special day. You are special and unique. This day is special, and you have been allowed to be a part of this grand day.

Look around you as you walk the streets of your neighborhood. Look around as you travel to the store to purchase some needed item. Stop for a moment, and take in the smells and sounds of the day. You are looking at people and things that you have never seen before. You are seeing sights and sounds that you have never heard before. You have been selected. You have been chosen to see the light in the sky and feel the air that is around you. You have been selected today to enjoy the beauty of life. Don't take life for granted. You have been chosen to have life today, and you are special. Walk in that anointing today, and know that you have been granted and given a true gift. Don't waste it with arguing about things that will be long forgotten and forgiven down the road.

JANUARY 19

~Day 19~

True Friendship

I am talking from my window today about having a deep and true friendship. Do you have people in your life whom you can share things with in truth and without any pretense? Do you have someone in your life whom you can call up and just talk about nothing in your life? Do you have someone you can trust with your most intimate secrets? Do you have someone in your life with whom you can share your deepest dreams? Do you have someone in your life with whom you can have the tough conversations about serious matters? If you don't, you are missing out on a great slice of living.

If you don't have someone who fills that corner of your life, I have a suggestion for you today. Jesus Christ would love to enter into a true friendship with you. Today and every day, He can be the Person in your life whom you can tell all your dreams, fears, doubts, and celebrations. Check out His friendships with His disciples.

JANUARY 20

~Day 20~

Privilege

When I looked out my window this morning, I had the privilege of seeing snow fall from the heavens and seeing rain hit the treetops. I had the privilege this morning of hearing the rain fall on my windowpanes and on the rooftop of my home. What a privilege it is to have sight and sound! We take far too many things for granted in this life. We think that we can just look out of our windows and we will see whatever our minds guide us to take in. We think that we can just pick up a book and just start to read it wherever and whenever we desire. We hear conversations and sounds, and we expect to hear things at the volume that we like. We are not entitled to these special gifts from God. We did not earn them and are not due them as a right. The gift of sight and sound is indeed a privilege. We need to stop and think about all the little and big gifts that our Heavenly Father has given us. We should stop right now and thank God for the gift of eternal life. We should hit the pause button right now and say, *"Thank you, Father, for everything!"* Good, now didn't that feel great?

Remember, we are only on this earth for a fleeing moment in time. We need to truly enjoy the privileges that He gives us in the here and now. Check out what the book of James says about time and life.

JANUARY 21

~Day 21~

Unsure

Are you unsure of yourself today? Are you wondering or doubting something in your life? Are you unsure of the path you should take on a certain job, idea, or unknown situation? You might be wondering if you truly have any impact on a given situation. I don't know what may be going on in your life at this very moment in time. I know some things for sure. I am convinced and certain that God is on His throne today. I know that Jesus Christ lives and that He will return to claim His disciples. I know for certain that my sins have been forgiven. I know that God is a loving God and that He loves you today.

I know that I am to share with you that we have a cloud of witnesses cheering for us to win our battles. I know that things may look down or unsure today, but God's angels are all around us. We think sometimes that the battle is lost or over. The devil is a liar. Don't believe that craziness in your mind. The battle is not over until our Heavenly Father has declared it to be so. If you are unsure of your path today, you only have to do one thing. Check out Ephesians chapter six. Ask God for His guidance and direction.

JANUARY 22

~Day 22~

Hospitals

I am grateful for the ability to walk, talk, and eat without any additional assistance. As I walk the halls of the hospital, I see so many sick people. We forget sometimes how blessed we are in this life. If you are feeling disappointed, discouraged, or down on yourself today, I have a great suggestion for you to give some serious consideration. I have a great pickup for you. Why not take a drive to your local hospital? Park your car and go inside. Look around at the people in the lobby, and just see the needs of the people. Take a moment and really look around the environment. Trust me, I bet your personal situation just got better. Pray about volunteering to assist in some way to help in your community. Hospitals are excellent places to learn about life and community. We are all called to minister to the sick and the needy.

JANUARY 23

~Day 23~

Traveling

I have been traveling a bit more than usual. I recently visited New York City and utilized the public transit system to get around town. I had the pleasure of observing many interesting sights and sounds within the train stations. As I entered the stairwell of one subway station, I heard the sounds of a woman singing her heart away. She sang old love songs that I knew from the fifties and sixties. Priceless music. Amazing. At the entrance of another subway train, I heard the beating of drums. Unbelievably beautiful—I felt like I was in a concert hall surrounded by a thousand sets of drums. I have heard angels singing on my train rides into Brooklyn Heights. I have seen and observed people on the train share with great passion the gospel of Jesus Christ. Amazing grace. Amazing love. Look out of your window today, and as you travel, look for the beauty of God's creation. You don't have to be down, disjointed, or disappointed today. Look around you, and see the beauty of the day. You might find it on a train ride.

JANUARY 24

~Day 24~

Delight

I look out my window, and the first thing that comes to mind is to be delighted with this day. Delight in the day, no matter how dark it looks outside. "Delight" means to take pleasure in this new day. Appreciate what is in front of you and what is in store for you today. This is a brand-new day, and yesterday is long gone. Don't dwell on the issues of yesterday, because we cannot not change any of yesterday's woes or victories. We have a new day in front of us. We spend far too much time dwelling on the past and agonizing about the future that we don't just enjoy today. I had to work hard at slowing down my pace to appreciate what is right in front of me. My prayer today is that you learn this lesson early in life. Jesus was trying to teach His disciples to be present in the moment. The disciples were always worrying about things, and Jesus was just about living in the present. I believe Jesus delighted in the present day. Jesus knew who would take care of Him and everyone else. We need to learn to walk in the joy, gladness, and delight of each new day.

JANUARY 25

~Day 25~

Jesus Loves Me

A few days ago, I was in a melancholy mood about some things that have happened in my life. I am normally a very positive person, but I could not shake this dark sense in my being. You ever feel like that? Well, I read and wrote down some scriptures. These spiritual disciplines helped, but my spirit was still melancholy. I knew that I needed to break this cloud and get back into a positive light. I was reading an article, and I saw an old song that I used to sing in church. You remember? "Jesus loves me, this I know, 'because the Bible tells me so." You remember that little song. Well, I started to sing the song and knew at that moment that Jesus loved me. He loves you today and every day. Sometimes, we need reminders. Sometimes, when we are going through periods of darkness and the mourning of losses, we just need a whisper. We will go through some days and nights of darkness, but as it says in the scripture, we will weep in the night, but joy will come in the morning. The light will shine in us and around us. Jesus loves you today and every day. I know because He loves me.

JANUARY 26

~Day 26~

Trailblazers

Have you ever been a trailblazer before? A trailblazer is a pioneer who is doing something for the first time, and everyone is watching to see how they will complete the task. I have been a trailblazer several times in my life. I can tell you that it is never warm and comfortable. I can tell you that being a catalyst can cause and create burnout in your life. The journey can also create great joy and accomplishment. The position of pioneer and leader can at times be very lonely. My mother and grandmother were true trailblazers. My mother told me that she picked one hundred pounds of cotton a day, and my grandmother picked three hundred pounds. Amazing. My mother was the first in her family to go to college. She was a trailblazer. My mom made it easier for me to go to school because she guided the way. When I was in a difficult spot in any of my assignments, I would look to my Heavenly Father for guidance. I felt that He put me in the assignment, and I truly believed with all my heart that He would see me through. Walk in His anointing today and every day.

JANUARY 27

~Day 27~

Blessing

As I look out my window this morning, I wonder where will this day take me? I ponder and wonder at the newness of the day. I know that I need to be a blessing to someone. I need to let someone know that they do indeed matter in this life. We need to lift our sisters and brothers up in love and prayer. We speak far too many negative words to one another and into the air. Speak joy and love to the ones closest to you today. We forget that we need to sometimes share verbally our appreciation of one another. We take our family and friends for granted. Be careful. Treat people the way that you want to be treated. Treat individuals with respect and love. Encourage someone with a compliment, with a call or card, or with a visit. Bless someone with a visit today! You will be a blessing and will be blessed.

JANUARY 28

~Day 28~

On the Train Again

Good morning, and blessings to you! I trust that wherever you are today, whether at work or play, that it is indeed a blessed day! Remember, yesterday is in the past and in your rearview mirror. We only truly have this very moment. I am traveling on the metro today. I am excited about the journey because I will be seeing so many different people. At every station that the train stops, new people will get on the train. So many amazing people from so many backgrounds and cultures. I love riding the train because it reminds me of the beauty of God's creation. Riding the train reminds me of what heaven might look like in the future. So many different groups of people. Enjoy the day, and take in the sights and sounds of this special day. Keep moving, because the train of life is moving, and you don't want to miss any of your appointed train stops.

JANUARY 29

~Day 29~

Elevators

I have a confession to make to you today from the window of life. I don't particularly care for elevators. I feel a bit closed in as people pile into every corner of the elevator. People just keep coming in without any consideration for weight capacities or personal space concerns. I feel closed in when I am in small confined spaces. I watched a woman in a wheelchair experience part of my anxiety. She was so uncomfortable that she was verbally talking to herself and trying to soothe her emotional distress. My heart ached for her. More people were trying to enter the elevator, and they pushed up against her wheelchair. As the elevator came to the final destination, the woman and I both exited at the same time. This woman daily traveled this elevator. She could not walk up the stairs and had to daily face her fears of enclosed spaces. She helped me with my elevator anxiety. She showed me an excellent example of moving forward with your life, even when things are not always easy or comfortable. Her goal was to get to work on time and be engaged in society. What anxiety is stopping you from moving forward with your next goal in life? Stop. Look around and take it to Jesus. He can help us.

JANUARY 30

~Day 30~

Stay Positive

Situations can happen so quickly; one minute you are up, and the next minute you are down. Life can and will throw some hard choices and rocks your way. Stay positive in your lane of life. Don't allow the negative things that come your way to poison you against people or life. I had a friend who was in a close relationship with someone, and they broke up. My friend was devastated after the breakup and turned bitter about people and life. Don't allow your spirit to become a bitter pill. She only saw life from a negative point of view. Don't live your life that way. So many times, we want to just read the Psalms in the Bible and just the ones that talk about joy. The scriptures also talk about the trials, the hurts, and the tribulations we will experience here on earth. I think about the apostle Paul and how he described in the scriptures, what he went through in life. Check it out in 2 Corinthians, and you will see that no matter what, Paul stayed positive. You want to know how he stayed so positive on his journey? Simple. He believed in the Lord his Savior, and he knew that the Holy Spirit journeyed with him. The Holy Spirit can and will journey with us today. Just ask. Stay positive.

JANUARY 31

~Day 31~

Live in Hope

I trust that you are living in hope today. Hope is many things to many people. Life can throw many different curves. Do you know what I mean when I say that? Life is an adventure. Some periods of time can be wonderful and without strain or pain. Other times in life, we will experience deep bouts of difficulties filled with terror, pain, and hurt. I want to share something with you on this last day of January. This day will never return again. Do not give up the hope that has been deposited in you. Don't give up on all the beauty of life due to some unexpected challenges thrown your way. Believe in the concept of eternal life, and live with the expectation of future promise and optimism. Don't look through life as if you don't have potential or faith. Look through life with hope of the One who is the Living Hope. Jesus said that He would never leave us nor forsake us in this world, or in the next. Live and walk in hope today and every day.

FEBRUARY 1

~Day 32~

Curves

At an unexpected hour, you received a phone call that changed the course of your life. You have been thrown a curve. A curve is a twist or unexpected event or fork in the road. A curve is something that can challenge our faith strongholds and cause us to seek higher ground. In some of our lives, many different curves have taken place. You expected to go in a certain direction in your life, and in a blink of an eye, your world changed. I remember sitting in the hospital room with my mom, being with her when she took her last breath on this earth. What a curve! What a twist to my world! I struggled and had to depend solely on my Lord and Savior, as it says in the scriptures: New International Bible, in Psalm 27:1-2"The Lord is my light and my salvation. Whom shall, I fear? The Lord is my stronghold, of whom shall I be afraid." Whatever curve you may be facing today, know that you walk under the protection of our Lord and Savior. Do not fear, and do not be afraid.

FEBRUARY 2

~Day 33~

Racing Thoughts

Do you ever have any racing thoughts in your head? Have things gone out of control in your mind? I have a suggestion for you today. It is one that I have been using, and it is working. My suggestion is to start to recite a psalm from the Bible out loud. You will be amazed what the sacred word of God will do for a racing mind. In the past few days, I have had many racing thoughts, and I have kept Psalm 27 close to my mind and heart: Review this Psalm today and you will be changed in your heart, mind, and soul. It is amazing how those words have calmed my mind, my heart, and my soul. Try it. I totally believe it will calm your racing thoughts.

FEBRUARY 3

~Day 34~

Waves

Sometimes things come into our lives like ocean waves that rise and fall in rapid succession. Every time you turn around, you find a new crisis hitting your door. Bang! You don't have a chance to catch your breath from the last wave of events. Bang! Another wave. You wonder in your mind, *is this only happening to me?* Perhaps you are in the middle of several major and difficult waves of sorrow and disappointment. You have a pity party of woes for yourself. Stop right there, and don't stay on that pity train. I want you to remember the next time you feel your emotions in a crashing wave crisis: Jesus told us in the scriptures that He would never leave us alone. He is with us through all situations in our live. He is with us through the waves. Forget about having a pity party and sending out pity invitations.

FEBRUARY 4

~Day 35~

Don't Waste

Don't waste another moment on craziness. Don't waste another moment on "what ifs." Don't waste another breath on regrets. Don't waste another moment on being unhappy with your life. Don't waste another moment feeling sorry for yourself. Don't waste time stewing over things that you cannot change. Don't waste another moment spending extra time on Facebook and wondering why someone "defriended" you. Trust me, that is truly a waste of time. Get on with your life, and enjoy the moment. Get on with your life, and experience growth in your life. Get on with your life, and be thankful that you have a life. Life is a true gift from God. Don't waste time with needless things in life. Get yourself together, and stop wasting precious time.

FEBRUARY 5

~Day 36~

Grateful

I am grateful for each day that I can walk and talk unassisted. What about you today? What are you grateful for in life? Is it a job? You got the one that you wanted, but it no longer keeps you satisfied. Is it a relationship that you wanted so badly? You got the person that you were interested in, but now you are taking the relationship for granted? Is it a home, car, or thing? The item is no longer "new," not as exciting? Take a moment, and check yourself. Remember to be grateful and appreciative of the blessings that have been bestowed upon you today. Time causes us to forget sometimes to be grateful.

FEBRUARY 6

~Day 37~

Keep Stepping

I want to give you a special note today. When you are feeling down, you have to keep stepping. You have to keep moving and keep stepping. Every day and every season are not going to be a picnic or a rose garden. You have to keep stepping in life and not allow yourself to have a pity party. You are a child of the King, and you have to continue even in difficult times. Hang in there. This, too, shall pass.

FEBRUARY 7

~Day 38~

Time Is Limited

Recently, I was riding in a hospital elevator with two complete strangers. As we descended, I spoke out loud and said, "I am getting to the know the halls, corridors, and exits of this hospital far too well. I am starting to learn the rhythm of this hospital." I did not know these people, and they did not know me, but for that one-minute, ride we contacted. Time is limited. I spoke about being in the urgent care unit and seeing so many the sick people. The woman shared that one minute she had a healthy husband, who had a minor stomachache, and was now diagnosed with stage four cancer. Time is limited. The man was devastated by what was happening with his family situation. We all realized at that very moment that time is limited and that our lives would be forever impacted. We all need to spend more time with our Lord and Savior.

FEBRUARY 8

~Day 39~

Should-Have, Could-Have Moments

Sometimes we live in a reality of "should have, could have." We think that we *should have* had a certain job or position. Did you ever stop and think that God could be sparing you from something or even from yourself? God knows our needs, wants, and desires far better than we do. He created us, remember. We have all had and will continue to have some future "should-have or could-have moments." I have learned that God knows my best future and that I needed to let go of those should-have or could-have moments. As I shared yesterday, time is limited, and I don't want to live in the land of regret and remorse. Do you? Why waste precious time? God knows what's best for our lives in the present.

FEBRUARY 9

~Day 40~

Downcast

In Psalm 42, the writer asks the question, "Why is my soul downcast?" He doesn't know the reason; he just knows that he is down and has a burden on his spirit. He says that he is deeply disturbed within his soul. I have been there, and will probably be there again. He answers his own question with the answer, "I will put my hope in God." When my soul is downcast, I seek the arms of my Lord and Savior. I have learned that I need to run to God when my soul is in a downcast mode. Learn this lesson from my window today. Run to Jesus, and He will lift your soul.

FEBRUARY 10

~Day 41~

New Morning

Today is a new morning. I look out my window, and I see life. I see the beauty of the world that God has given to me today. I am feeling blessed that I can see and hear and feel today. Do you sense His presence in your life today? Think for a moment, and embrace this thought. You can see and hear and taste. You can see color and movement and life. Don't take it for granted. God has been good to you. There have been some good times and some dark times, but God has always been there to see me through. He is here. He will see you through whatever tragedy you are going through today. We have to learn to trust that He will guide us, lead us, and instruct us each and every day. Today is a new morning. Forget the old, and embrace this new day with a new sense of direction in His heavenly embrace.

FEBRUARY 11

~Day 42~

Tired

Are you tired today? If you are tired, I have some advice for you. Slow down. Try to be patient with yourself. Try your best to focus on the positive and not the negative. When you are tired, the negative continually seems to come to the surface. Sing a song in your mind. Read a psalm out loud. Laugh at yourself. Hug yourself and be glad. Try to rejoice and be glad. Enjoy your day. Take care of yourself.

FEBRUARY 12

~Day 43~

Love Meaning

What does love mean to you? People? Things? Feelings? When you use the word *love*, what does it truly mean? What is love to you? To me, it is not so much about using the word *love*, but how we express and demonstrate love, by action and deed. I could write on the subject of love for the next one hundred years and still not cover every aspect of the word. Jesus Christ walked on this earth, and He loved us so much that He gave his life for us. Love is giving someone a glass of water or a cup of their favorite tea, without them asking for it or expecting something in return. Love is a word in my book that requires action. What are you doing today to show that you truly know and have the meaning of love in your heart and soul? Love requires positive light and action. Why not put some action with that *love* word today?

FEBRUARY 13

~Day 44~

Real Love

Do you know what real love is? Have you ever experienced real love? I am not talking about the kind of pretend love that actors act out in movies and television. I am talking about real love. Real love is kind. Real love is patient with one another. Real love remembers no wrongs or holds any grievances. Real love seeks no equal status because it is already in the core of the relationship. Do you know what real love is?

It is not the fake love that is one sided in a relationship. Fake love has to have all the attention or make all the decisions in a relationship. Fake love is unkind and unbending. Fake love remembers all the mistakes, slights, and hurts. Fake love is unforgiving.

Real love hurts when the other person hurts. Real love wants success equally for all parties involved. Real love is unafraid to move out into unknown and uncharted adventures. Real love will sacrifice for another party. Jesus Christ gives us examples of real love. He came on this earth and sacrificed His life for you and me. He touched our hearts, minds, and souls and taught us real love. As I look out my window today, I ask you to seek in your hearts to experience and demonstrate the real love of kindness, patience, and joy.

FEBRUARY 14

~Day 45~

Real Love Challenge

People spend millions and millions of dollars expressing their love to their loved ones. I have a better way of expressing love. Rather than spending all of those dollars, how about a real love challenge? Are you interested in taking this real challenge? To show and demonstrate real love, let's really listen to our loved ones and not dismiss something that they are saying. How about showing some real love and not having to have our way all the time? How about letting some things go and not mentioning them each time we have a disagreement? How about some real love—writing a little love note and placing it on his or her pillow? Even just a simple "I love you" and a smile will do. Just a thought from my window today on this love day!

FEBRUARY 15

~Day 46~

Check Ourselves

We sometimes need to check ourselves. We need to check how we treat the people we care about. We sometimes treat strangers better than family. We need to check ourselves in how we talk to individuals we love. Sometimes we can speak so harshly to the people we are supposed to love with our whole heart.

I was visiting a friend who lived in an apartment complex. As I passed by one of the apartment doors, I overheard someone shouting with a harsh tone. There was such hatred in the tone of the one speaking behind the door of the apartment. I asked my friend who lived in the next apartment. She responded that it was a very nice family and that they were so loving and kind to each other. I have since met the family, and you would never have known there was an issue. We need to check ourselves in how we talk to family, friends, and loved ones in and behind closed doors. It is something that I need to do more often. What about you?

FEBRUARY 16

~Day 47~

New Day

You will find the topic of a new day to be a recurring theme in this Daily Window. You want to know why? Each day is a gift, and each day is uniquely different. I look out my window, and I see the sun shining and the blue sky. Yesterday was dark, damp, and cold. I made some mistakes yesterday. Today has the potential of new starts and new beginnings. Today, we each have been given a new chance. A new day to right a wrong or a mistake. A new day to tell someone that they are special and a new day to sing a new song. A new day to recommit our hearts, minds, and souls to Jesus Christ. A new day to walk with Christ and grow in our relationship with Him. A new day for a new adventure.

FEBRUARY 17

~Day 48~

Special

Today is a special day. You want to know why? Because we have been allowed to wake up and be a part of this great day. We were on God's wake-up list today. At this moment right now, you have a memory of this day. You have a memory of this moment. Praise the Lord. Special is unique. You are unique and wonderful. Don't allow anything or anyone make you feel less than special and unique. You have been allowed to wake up and be a part of this great big world. What an amazing gift we have been given! Don't waste it, my friend. You have a part to play in this day. Embrace the day, and move on with your life. Shake off the stresses, worries, and hurts of yesterday. Today is a new day. It is special because we have never seen this day before. It is special because we can change our ways, our outlooks, and our whole essence. We are specially and wonderfully made. Enjoy your day.

FEBRUARY 18

~Day 49~

Complicated

We do not exist in a perfect world. People are going to challenge us. Our children are going to be difficult and give us a run for every ounce of parenting skill we have ever learned. Our jobs will be frustrating and challenging. Our marriages are going to be tested by both inside and outside forces. We are human beings, and we are learning to navigate on this great planet. Catch the daily wisdom for today. If we seek the guidance of Jesus every day, in all of our lives' daily decisions, I know for a fact that our lives will be less complicated. Jesus taught the principle of love. If we love more, trust me—life would truly be less complicated. If we allow the Holy Spirit to guide us and to instruct us, we will be in less complicated situations. Try it and see.

FEBRUARY 19

~Day 50~

Life

I ponder life. I have to be honest that as I get older, the more I value life. I don't take life for granted any longer. I don't just assume that I am going to be present on this earth later today. I don't take it for granted that I am going to be here tomorrow. I don't want to take anything for granted in all of my relationships. I have found that life is just too short. I don't want to clutter my precious time with craziness and regret. I have found as I have grown older that I am more sensitive to words spoken to me. Words carry great meanings. Please don't take this day for granted. Live the day in the fullness of the Lord! Don't get caught up in foolish and negative thoughts, views, and actions. Live the day under the guidance and direction of the Holy Spirit. If you follow His instructions, you will have a better day and life. Read God's word daily. Trust me. I know.

FEBRUARY 20

~Day 51~

He Still Speaks

People wonder and argue about whether or not God stills speaks to us today. Some folks believe that God only spoke doing the days of the scriptures, and others say He speaks only to certain people. I believe that He is continually reaching out to us. I believe that He still speaks to us. We need to only listen. He still guides us, instructs us, teaches us, and encourages us. The other day I was in New York City for an extremely important appointment. Prior to going to the meeting, I saw a book on my friend's table. It was a book that my friend would generally not have in their home. I had the same book on encouragement. I didn't remember bringing the book with me.

The next day, I asked my friend if I had given her a copy of the book for Christmas. She replied that she had received a pamphlet in the mail and had ordered the book. I was shocked. God showed me that He was speaking to both of us. He was an Encourager to both of us through this particular book. We needed to reminded to be faithful to Him. He is still speaking. Listen to His messages today. He still speaks.

FEBRUARY 21

~Day 52~

Don't Stress

As I look out my window on this beautiful winter morning, the message of the day is *chill out*. We spend far too much of our time stressing over things that will never happen in life. Our minds have such great imaginations that we sometimes send them into overdrive. Don't stress about tomorrow. You want to know why? One, you are not there yet. Two, you don't own tomorrow yet. Three, you have enough on your plate with today's life concerns. We need to learn how to enjoy this day. Keep moving forward with life today. Enjoy this day, as it is a special and unique day. You only have today. You have been allowed to walk, breathe, and live today. This is a gift of life. Don't waste it by stressing about things that you truly can't change.

FEBRUARY 22

~Day 53~

Journaling

I have a question for you: Do you want to grow and learn more about yourself? Do you want to grow spiritually? Do you want to stop making the same mistakes over and over again in life? Well, try journaling for the first time, or pick it up again with a renewed interest. I started journaling years ago after a friend kept nagging me about how much I would grow to love it. She was so right on. I now love to journal. However, I have to be honest: it was a chore in the beginning. Recently, I randomly picked up one of my earlier journals, and I started to scan some of the pages. I was overcome with a thankful heart that God had answered so many of my prayers throughout the years. I didn't remember. I was blown away with memories of people, opportunities, and situations. In my journal, I saw not only my own personal growth but the spiritual growth of many of my family and friends. Try it, and you might end up having a great time with it.

FEBRUARY 23

~Day 54~

Woke Up

I have a question for you today: Who woke you up this morning? Who allowed you to wake up this morning? You woke up this morning to start fresh and new. You woke up and were given a second chance to start over again. You might have made some mistakes yesterday. Yes? No? You might have said some hurtful things or thought the wrong thoughts. You woke up to a new start button. You woke up to a new day of grace, mercy, and love. You woke up to a new day of forgiveness, and forgetting the wrongs of the past and the regrets of yesterday. Praise the Lord. You woke up today. Make the most of this glorious day in the Lord! Wake up and praise the Lord, who is worthy to be praised today! He woke you up today.

FEBRUARY 24

~Day 55~

Let Go

Good morning. New day. New attitude. Let go. Let go of whatever is holding you back from what your purpose is today. Let go of the regrets of yesterday. You have been holding on to burdens that should have long ago been buried. Why are you still carrying them on your shoulders today? Let go. You cannot change the past; you can only live in the present moment. You don't own the future. Enjoy this day. Live this day in the presence of God. Talk with Jesus about the struggles you have been carrying on your shoulders. He will whisper in your ear, if you will listen, "My yoke is easy, and my burden is light." You have added so much stuff to your life that is totally unnecessary. Listen to me: really turn everything over to God, and let go of everything that keeps you tangled. I know I had to let go of a lot of baggage. Free at last. Thank God I am free at last! Let go and let God handle it, and then you will be able to sing the tune "Free at Last."

FEBRUARY 25

~Day 56~

Trials and Challenges

Make no mistake: you will have trials and challenges in your life. You already know that. Why does it surprise us when things happen to us? We must go into the shock mode of thinking in our minds. However, we must realize that every day is not going to be peace free. We would love for that to happen, but you know what? That's not real. Life can and will be complicated at times. We will have periods in our lives when we will go through seasons of trials and challenges. No one looks forward to these periods in our lives. I will say several things about these times of trials and challenges. We grow as individuals. We think about more than ourselves during these periods. We don't take life for granted when we are waiting for lab tests to come back. We will have trials and challenges when our relatives and friends come down with illnesses that require additional care. Walk with God, and He will carry you through all of your trials and challenges today and forever.

FEBRUARY 26

~Day 57~

Hard Times

Yesterday in the Daily Window, I was sharing about all the trials and challenges that we can and will face in this life. I want to continue today with that particular theme. It is only natural that we want to concentrate on just good things and good times. However, I don't want us to miss out on all the things that we can learn from the hard times. I think about the early Christians and how they learned to develop fortitude and perseverance through their struggles and challenges. We learn patience through our difficult and hard times. If we allow ourselves, we can be changed and transformed during these periods. I looked the other day at some of my old journals, and I can see changes within myself. I see the impact that my hard times have had on my life and how I have grown closer to my Lord and Savior. I trust Him more and more every day. He carried me through some pretty tough times, and He will carry you through your struggles and crises. Trust Him, as weeping endures for a night but joy truly comes in with the morning light.

FEBRUARY 27

~Day 58~

Be Prepared

The way to endure whatever is coming our way today is to be prepared. What I mean by being prepared is being ready and equipped to handle anything. You could ask, "How do I prepare or equip myself for the unknown events that could happen in my life today?" Great question, and I have a great answer. Have you forgotten to put on your spiritual armor today? Have you moved so quickly and rushed out of the house without spending time with God this morning? Have you forgotten to eat your spiritual food? Go check out Ephesians 6:10–18; learn those verses and believe in them every day. Trust me. You will be prepared for whatever might come your way. I don't leave my home until I put on my spiritual armor. I want to be prepared for whatever comes my way today. I will not be afraid, because my Lord and Savior is leading the way and protecting me from the darts and arrows that will surely come my way. Be prepared.

FEBRUARY 28

~Day 59~

Friendships

Early this morning, I spoke with a friend whom I have known for over thirty years. She is in the mission field halfway around the world. The timing of our conversation was her night and my day. We are several time zones apart from one another. We were talking just like we were in the same room. It was a continuation of a conversation that started over thirty years ago, and it continues to this day. It is the same conversation with continually new dimensions. We hold each other accountable by asking questions about our spiritual journey. Questions like, did you check with God on this? Do you have peace? Are you where you are supposed on this part of the journey? Deep, soulful conversations. Check out Proverbs 17:17 regarding the significance of a friend—powerful words today.

FEBRUARY 29

~Day 60~

Isolation

We were not created to live in isolation from one another. We were created to be in fellowship with God and with each other. Isolation is separation, segregation, and loneliness. Isolation breeds several things that I see in many people. Isolation breeds and leads to loneliness, which can lead to depression. We were created for friendship and fellowship. Don't isolate yourself from people. If you have been hurt by folks and you want to swear off people, rebuke that thought from your mental intake. To isolate from society and interaction is what I call "stinky thinking." If you have been hurt, pick yourself up and brush yourself off, and get back into the game of life. God created us for fellowship. Get out today and try to make a new friend. There are close to eight billion people on this great planet, and I am sure there are a few folks here for you and me. Try it and you may make a new friend today.

MARCH 1

~Day 61~

Snowing in March

When I was reading my Bible, I read an exciting story about a hero fighting a lion down in a pit on a snowy day. Check it out in 2 Samuel chapter 23. It's amazing what can happen in the snow. What is your day like on a snowy day in March, just before the arrival of springtime? I am blessed to be in my house and thankful that I have a home. I am grateful to God for heat, safety, and warm clothes. I am grateful for a rooftop that is safe and sound. I am thankful to God for His many mercies and His amazing love. I am thankful for everything that the Lord had done and continues to do for us on a snowy day in March. What about you? What are you thankful for today?

MARCH 2

~Day 62~

Snowing in March-Part II

It is still snowing on this beautiful day in March. The snow looks beautiful. Neither the squirrels nor the birds are around in the neighborhood today. It continues to be very quiet in the neighborhood. I am amazed at the beauty of nature and how God is taking care of everything. Sometimes, it is good to stop and just give thanks for everything that His hands have made. I don't know your struggles today, but allow God's presence into your life, and He will see you through all types of seasons in life. It is snowing today, but spring is just around the corner.

MARCH 3

~Day 63~

Anniversary Date

Today is a key anniversary date in my life. An anniversary date is when something is marked as special and significant in your life. You are changed forever by this date and the event that took place. This date is the day that my mom, one of the greatest women who ever lived on this earth, took her last breath on this side of life. I was with my mom at the hospital when she passed from this life to the next.

    I was standing by the side of her bed. I leaned down toward her bed and said to her, "I love you, Mom." I really didn't expect any response. My mom had not verbally spoken for several days. The doctors said it was just a matter of time. I was standing, and all of a sudden, she responded, "I love you too." I was shocked.

    What a privilege God had given me to share in that moment with my mom. Our last Daily Window together. I will always be thankful and grateful for that special opportunity. I will never forget that moment. I am extremely grateful to my mom for sharing all our Daily Window sessions together.

MARCH 4

~Day 64~

Quiet Place

I am at a cancer hospital today with my sister for her treatment. I have come with her to hopefully be a comfort at this very difficult time in her life. A cancer treatment room can be a very lonely place at times. The walls can close in on you. I wanted my sister to know that she was not alone in her battle and that she had strong prayer covering her. She was tired from being at the hospital waiting for a blood transfusion all day the day before. My sister was given some medication to help her tolerate the day's procedures better. As I sat in the treatment room, I started to notice that there were many treatment rooms. They were full of people, but there were limited conversations. As I watched and observed, I said to myself, *this is a perfect time to pray.* "Lord, please be with every family represented here in this space. Allow your Holy Spirit to touch each soul in this place and fill them with your holy peace and joy."

As you are going about your day today, look for a quiet place to pray for family, friends, church, country, and strangers along the way. Be an encouragement to someone today.

MARCH 5

~Day 65~

Discernment

I am in the middle of making a critical and important decision regarding my commitment to a future project. I have a tendency to lean toward the negative and not to want to commit to new opportunities. My natural inclination is to stay in my own comfort zone. However, when I allow God to direct and instruct, my life improves beyond my wildest dreams. I trust God. I know that He will lead me and guide me to places that I never knew or experienced. The best advice I can give you from my windowsill today is to bring everything to God, and He will guide you. Trust God today. He will give you heavenly wisdom and discernment.

MARCH 6

~Day 66~

Miracles Still Happen

Miracles still happen. Recently, my husband and I took a road trip to New York. We had stayed a couple of days with a relative and were getting ready to return home. My husband left the apartment to carry some of our luggage to the car. It always takes more than one trip to the car for my stuff. My husband returned to the apartment and asked me for a couple of dollars. I started to look for my wallet in my backpack and could not find it.

As I continued my search, my husband handed me my wallet. I was surprised. He informed me that when he went to put our bags in the car, the doorman said that someone had found my wallet. Miracles still happen. I was shocked. My money and my credit cards were still in the wallet. Nothing was out of place. I was in a part of the city where people take anything and everything from your car. No one would have known if he had just slipped my wallet in his pocket. Miracles still happen. God's grace is still on the earth. There are still honest people who walk on this great planet. The Lord said that He would never leave nor forsake us. I needed a miracle yesterday, and He gave me one.

MARCH 7

~Day 67~

Lenten Season

When I woke up this morning, I was grateful to God for life. He is my miracle. I am thinking during this Lenten season, *what do I give to Jesus?* Over the years, I have given up bread, candy, gum, and a host of other things. What about my internal stuff? I try to give up the negative thoughts, opinions, or conclusions about people or things. I have not been successful with the internal parts of my soul. The dark clouds of my mind continue to hinder the great possibilities of life. I made up my mind. I will give to Jesus all my internal negative things and conclusions. I will, with the help of His miracles, keep the dark clouds at bay. What are you doing to improve your spiritual way with God doing this Lenten season? Just checking—think about it.

MARCH 8

~Day 68~

Be Alert

In the scriptures, we are told be alert. Yesterday, I shared that I was giving to God all my negative thoughts. Last night, I was in a battle to keep my thought life and prayer life positive. Be alert when you make a vow or commitment. The enemy knows human nature, and he knows that we want to be closer to God. The evil one will do whatever it takes to distract us from reaching our spiritual goals. I am thankful that God is with us every step of the way on this journey. I refused to allow the evil one to have access to my thought life. It is truly a battlefield of the mind. I chose God. I chose to stay alert and move under the influence and guidance of the Holy Spirit. I will stay alert today. What about you? What do you need to do to be alert for today in your life? Do a spiritual assessment on yourself, and be alert today and every day.

MARCH 9

~Day 69~

Personal Self-Care

I woke up exhausted. Did you ever feel like that on the start of a new day? Not a good feeling, my friend. My head felt as though it was under water all the time, even on dry land. As I shared in an earlier Daily Window, I gave up all negative thinking for the Lenten season. I am trying to change my internal actions and grow deeper spiritually in my walk with God. Knowing that I was already tired from the start of today's race, I made a mental note to myself to do more personal self-care. We don't treat our bodies and minds to enough personal self-care. Are you tired, frustrated, disappointed, or discouraged today? Take a moment and think about something small that will give you rest and joy today. You need to do more self-care. Today, I left a meeting early and just came home. I have just finished brewing a special pot of my favorite tea. I plan to sit down by my favorite window and take some time sipping tea and thanking God for His goodness. Why don't you take some time today and do some personal self-care?

MARCH 10

~Day 70~

Unexpected Gift

I received an unexpected gift today from God. A gift that totally touched my heart and soul. Totally unexpected and totally undeserved. I didn't deserve this gift of love, and it was fully given with nothing expected in return. I will remember this day deep down in my soul. God touched my heart, mind, soul, and body. God also gave us another gift. He gave us the gift of His Son, Jesus Christ. We didn't earn the gift of Jesus. We don't deserve the gift of Jesus. We were given the gift of Jesus's love unconditionally. If you think about this, we are getting a gift every day—the gift of the love of Jesus, an unexpected gift. We will one day be with Jesus in a world that lives totally on peace, love, hope, and joy. Take a moment right now, and reflect on God's gifts to you. Unexpected gifts of love.

MARCH 11

~Day 71~

Take a Moment

Take a moment. Catch what I am about to say. Take a moment. Look around you and really take a look at your surroundings. This is a new day. I talk a lot about the theme of a new day. You want to know why I talk about this subject so much? It is because everyone takes time for granted. Somehow, in our minds or hearts, we think that we are due to wake up in the mornings. We think that time is somehow owed to us. We think that time exists only for us. I don't know where we get this sense of entitlement. Well, I would have to say, "Take a moment and hear this: no day is due to you." We did not earn a new day, and we cannot earn a new day. We did not create tomorrow, and we don't have the ability to create today. Take a moment and thank God for this beautiful day.

MARCH 12

~Day 72~

A Door of Stress

I have shared with family and friends not to allow a door of stress to come into their presence. You control what and who comes into your house. We open ourselves up to anxiety and worry that may never happen, but this stress leaves us with a troubled soul. My suggestion to you today is to not allow your mind or your heart to even entertain a door of stress. When we allow stress in our minds, it robs us of our joy. When we have a door of stress on us, we begin to feel uneasy and out of place. If you are stressed about your future plans, check out Proverbs 16:9. Spend some time with this scripture verse, and I pray that it will lessen your door of stress.

MARCH 13

~Day 73~

We Are Called

Recently, I was having a down day, and I came across Isaiah chapter 43. This word is for you today and every day. God loves us. He has called us, and we are His. If someone tells you that you are nothing, and that you have no meaning, please don't receive that message in your spirit. Words can have power over us. We play words over and over again in our minds. I want to let you know, from my Daily Window, that holy scriptures have power. God says we are His. You have a purpose and a calling. Check out the scripture. Read one verse and it will set you on the right course for the day. Trust me. I believe everyone has a calling or purpose in this life.

MARCH 14

~Day 74~

Open Files

The other day I had a terrible headache. Let's just say, it was not a good day. I realized that I had too many open files in my mind. I was thinking about too many things that were distracting me from the present moment. I had too many unresolved open files in my head. You ever feel that way? Your mind just racing? We have no release until we hit the delete or the save buttons of our minds. I had allowed too many open files to ruin my state of mind. If you want to walk in peace today, close down some of those open files now. Hit the delete button. Check out your open files, and do a needed purge.

MARCH 15

~Day 75~

Listening

When was the last time you took some time to just chill out? We rush from place to place. Take a moment and really listen to your inner self. Do you ever really listen to yourself? Are you too busy with life's events to listen to your inner body and spirit? It is important to take some time and focus on what our minds, hearts, and bodies are trying to communicate to us. My body said to me that I needed to take a day off from everything. I now listen to my body and take time. I decided to take the whole day off and just rest in the Lord. When was the last time you listened to your body? Take a moment to really listen, and perhaps you need to get in a quiet space. When was the last time you spent some really quiet time with the Creator? Hey, what about today? What about right now?

MARCH 16

~Day 76~

Rest

Good morning! (Or is it good evening for you?) Whatever time of the day or night that you happen to be reading this Daily Window, how did you sleep last night? Did you have a restful sleep? When was the last time you got a great night's sleep? Something to think about for a moment, isn't it? I believe that being sleep deprived is a growing crisis in this country. We have far too many people not sleeping well. You need more rest. Do you know why you are not sleeping well? When was the last time you had an annual checkup? Think about spending a little more time in freeing up your soul. Think about spending a little more time with God instead of having so many missed appointments with Him.

MARCH 17

~Day 77~

Seasons

A season is a period of time. We will go through different seasons in our lives. In the scriptures, it talks about a time to live and a time to die. A time to laugh and a time to cry. I am beginning to learn what season of life I am in now. God is continually teaching me my seasons and my times. I pray that I become a quick study and know when to move and when to stay in a season. To know when to plant and when to harvest. I have looked back on some events in my life, and I wish that I had known more about my seasons. I thank God for teaching me about some of my seasons of life. Take some time with the Heavenly Father today, and learn about some of your seasons. You may come away from your talk with God learning some critical life lessons.

MARCH 18

~Day 78~

Woke Up

Have you ever woken up in the middle of the night and couldn't go back to sleep? It happened to me the other night, and I just couldn't get back into a comfortable space. All of a sudden, my cell phone makes a sound, and my youngest daughter was texting me. She had never texted me that late before. I immediately picked up my phone thinking that something was wrong. She said in her text that she could not sleep. I asked if everything was okay, and she said yes. I responded that I would pray that we both could get some needed sleep. A few minutes later, my eldest daughter joined the early morning party of being awake. I have to say it was pretty special that they both texted me and that they both were safe and just needed to chat. I woke up this early morning because I needed to pray for my family. I thank God for His many mercies.

    The next time you wake up in the middle of the night, I would like to suggest instead of complaining that you can't sleep, maybe it might be a time to have a conversation with our Heavenly Father. Maybe you woke up for a special reason. Maybe, it was time to spend time with Him. It says in the word of God that Jesus rose early to spend time with His Father. Check it out in the gospels of Mark and John.

MARCH 19

~Day 79~

Mixed Motives

Sometimes, we don't really know why we do the things that we do. What truly motives us to do the things that we do? We think in our minds that the things we do are for the good of all parties. We sometimes think that we are doing activities in the right spirit. Sometimes we are totally unsure, and we have mixed motives. When we experience this emotion in our lives, it is important to do a spiritual checkup on ourselves. It is important not to lie to yourself. The best way to find out the truth of a matter or situation is to ask the Lord for guidance and direction. Lord, am I doing this for the right reasons? Please give me understanding and direction. He will answer you and set you on the right side of the situation.

If you are unclear of your direction this day and you are unsure of your motives, seek God. Ask God. He will give you wisdom and direction. Check out the first chapter of James in the scriptures. Our brother James gives us ageless practical advice. Seek God. Trust God and your motives will become crystal clear.

MARCH 20

~Day 80~

Take a Moment

As I was traveling to church this morning, I looked up into the clear blue sky. What a moment. I was overcome with all the blessings that God has given me. I thought about my own mom and the amazing impact that she had on my life. She lived for only a short period of time on this present earth. I would now pay millions of dollars to sit at the kitchen window with her and hear her voice one more time. When I think of all the things that she imparted to me at that windowsill…I am humbled. As I go through life events now, many of my reflections come from my mom sharing with me, her pearls of godly wisdom and insight. Take a moment and reflect on your life. Take a moment and just look around at the beauty of the sky! Trust *God* to travel with you today! Take a moment.

MARCH 21

~Day 81~

Be Brave

Most days, after I came home from school and before I started to work, my mother and I would sit at the kitchen window. I looked forward to our times together. I loved my mom more than life. My mom seemed to find time for each of us, even when she became gravely ill. It was as if she wrote the book on parenting. She was the bravest woman whom I had ever met. She could not change her struggles, but she was determined to change her children's challenges. My mom did not allow any of her hardships, heartaches, craziness, or discrimination take away her joy of life. Keep moving forward and don't allow the situations in your life keep you from obtaining your God-given goals and talents. Don't allow anyone or anything take away your joy!

MARCH 22

~Day 82~

Moods

When I did not feel good about myself and when the whole world seemed to be going against me, I would have a conversation with my mom. Sometimes, she would agree with me that the world was not treating me right. Sometimes, she would say, "You think the whole world is against you; well, it is not! Get over it." I would laugh at that statement, and my world would be straight again. She was honest and that is a rare commodity today. People do not generally speak the truth. If you can, find friends and loved ones to speak truth in your life. Treasure them. I am talking about people who value you and do not want anything from you. Don't be put off by the craziness of this world nor by your own moods at the moment. Let the mood pass, and be careful with your thoughts, emotions, comments, and actions. Seek God. Trust God.

MARCH 23

~Day 83~

Forward

There are going to be days when you just feel "down." I remember a song, my mom used to sing sometimes: "There'll be days like this, yes, there'll be days like this." Every once in a while, you are going to feel what I call "out of sorts." You just don't feel right (whatever "right" is for you). It's different for each one of us; it's okay to be down for a day. Sometimes, it's good to process your emotions. But you cannot stay in that state. You have to kick the emotions out of your system. Shake off and continue to move on with life. Because you know what? Life is good.

You were blessed even before you were born into this world. Our emotions or feelings sometimes plays tricks on us. Our feelings tell us that "we are too this or too that." Don't play into the drama of emotions. Move forward. Think forward thoughts. Don't stop growing. Don't stop learning. Don't stop loving. Do look forward. It's important to keep stepping.

MARCH 24

~Day 84~

Breaks

Sometimes, we just need to take a break from everything! My mother was a very wise woman. She never had a problem with us children getting up in the morning for school or to go to work. You want to know why? She would allow us to take a break from school or work for no reason at all. She knew that sometimes, you just needed to get out of the daily routine of work, school, or life. I remember that once a school quarter, we could potentially take a day off from school, no questions asked. My mom was progressive. I just didn't realize that about her at the time. She was just my mom. Now, there were conditions to this day off. We had to be ahead in our schoolwork and activities. What happens when we take a break? We are able to refocus our energy and our thoughts and reconnect to what is important. Jesus did this. He would take some time out and get away from the craziness. Reconnect with his Father. Sometimes, we also need to quiet our soul and do some soul care. Just take some time not to be stressed nor tensed up in your head and mind. Start to learn to enjoy life.

MARCH 25

~Day 85~

Pity Parties

My mom did not believe in having an extended pity party for herself or anyone. It was okay to grieve a situation for a short period of time but never to wallow. How do I know that? Because of the way she lived her life. She never shared in any conversation that I ever held with her "that if only this would have happened, then this would be better." The only comment that she made in reference to her marriage status was that it was great the first seven years of marriage. Being raised in the South, my mom experienced a great deal of racism. She did not allow the institution of racism make her a victim, nor did she wear the scars of hatred. She did not allow it to contaminate her heart nor wear down her soul. Walk by faith and not by sight today and every day.

MARCH 26

~Day 86~

Scale

As I sit at my window in my rocking chair and watch the wind blow through the trees, I am trying to have an upbeat spirit in my soul. I am trying not to be down on myself or down on anyone or anything. What sent my thoughts in this direction? I know. I got on the scale this morning, and I had gained another three pounds. Where did those extra pounds come from? I refused to allow the scale to dictate my state of mind or being. I allowed negative scale results to influence my soul for too long and for too many years. There must be some type of mental term for people who get depressed over the "reading the scale mentality." If the scale is down, everything is wonderful. If the scale is up, everything is bad. I have decided to rebuke my negative thinking in the name of Jesus and move on with my day!

    I remember a thought that captured my thinking last year: "I will not allow the night clouds of my mind to rob me of the anticipated joy of the morning sunlight." Today, enjoy the moment and the future. Don't allow any night clouds of your minds rob you of the anticipated joy of the afternoon rays of life.

MARCH 27

~Day 87~

Sense

It certainly does not feel like spring yet! It is cold outside, and the wind continues to be a nuisance. We still need our winter coats. My mom could always sense when I was a little down in the dumps. Maybe it was the way I walked into the room or the inflection in my voice. She would look at me and assess what she should say to me at the right moment. You might not be sensing joy in what you are doing on your job right at this moment. Hang in there…change is coming. I can sense it. The wind is still here, but I truly sense that spring is just around the corner. One thing that I know for sure: God is on His throne today, and He sent his Son to bring joy, encouragement, light, and peace. Walk in that thought today!

MARCH 28

~Day 88~

Regrets

I can remember times when I was tense and frustrated with the way things were happening my life. "Everything was moving too slow"—or so I thought at the time. As I look back over my life, I regret that I took those frustrations out on my loved ones. I believe I did that because I felt safe and secure, that they would still love me unconditionally. They did. However, heaving the anger and frustration upon them was not the right thing to do.

I took it out on my mom the most. I should not have violated that sacred relationship with my own disappointments, issues, and uncertainties. She did not create my messes or problems. My mom refused to go with me on my roller-coaster ride of craziness. What a waste of time. I could have been creating better memories with her. We shared a lot of great memories, but we could have had far more. Enjoy your loved ones. It's okay to vent occasionally, but don't violate the love trust. Treasure the love and have fewer regrets. The only one who could truly help us with our issues is Jesus, and when we put *Him* first, all the rest will fall into place.

MARCH 29

~Day 89~

Wow

My mom was diagnosed with breast cancer, and it later metastasized into bone cancer. Pain management options were limited in 1975. She never complained during her five-year cancer battle, even though she was in constant pain. Even when the experiential surgery and drugs did not work, she never succumbed to a pity party. She once said shortly before she died that she prayed that the pain that she was suffering, her children would never have to experience, and that she hoped and prayed that she carried all of our suffering in her pain. Wow. She walked with God every day. We need to take everything to God in prayer. Wow.

MARCH 30

~Day 90~

Good Friday

Recently, my sister and I were sharing memories regarding Good Friday and how we had to behave in our home on that particular day. My mom taught us early in our home to be respectful of the day, and she shared with us that this day would have enormous impact on our lives in the future. She was so right in her teachings. One of the rules that my mom established early on was that we had to be quiet on Good Friday from noon to three o'clock. I always remembered that quietness in a household with five children. Neither the radio nor the television was allowed to be on during those times. We were not allowed to go out and play with our friends. We could either read or write, but we needed to do it quietly. Jesus had to experience Friday to get to Sunday. We have to experience Friday (many times) to get to Sunday. To get restored and renewed! He is Risen! He is Risen indeed!

MARCH 31

~Day 91~

Racing and Rushing

I woke up late, and I discovered that I had overslept by an additional hour. I rushed out of bed. Rushed to brush my teeth. Rushed to do my devotionals. Rushed to put on my clothes. Rushed to get to into my car and rushed to get to the gym. I was running into the gym to get my spot in the classroom. (I didn't want anyone to be in *my spot*—as if I owned the space!) Out of the corner of my eye, I say my gym instructor in the parking lot. I said to myself, "This is crazy." This is a Saturday morning. A beautiful morning, and I was attempting to rush through the day! *Get ahold of yourself*, I said to myself.

    Yesterday, I had such a peace in my soul. Today, I am like a crazy lady. When you find that you happened to start your day racing and rushing, tell yourself to *calm down*, take a deep breath, and enjoy the rest of your day. That is what I decided to do with the rest of my day!

APRIL 1

~Day 92~

New Life

When I sing the song "He Lives," I sing with joy, belief, and adoration. I pray that you also sing it with joy, belief, and adoration today and every day! I know that He lives and I will see my Lord and Savior. He gave us the greatest gift: a second chance in life. A new life in Him. To have the assurance of being born again in Christ and to live eternally with our Heavenly Father. Do you have a new life in Christ? You can. All you have to do is ask.

APRIL 2

~Day 93~

Rest

When I was a little girl, sometimes my mom would get very quiet. I did not understand her needing this quiet time alone. I do understand now. She was busy raising a family and dealing with life issues. She just needed time alone to regroup. Sometimes, we all need time to rest, and if you need to get into a quiet space, just do it! Just take some time to rest in God today! Get into some quiet space and have a good time reading, watching TV, or just listening to a podcast. Know that you are loved and that you just need some rest today. Hang in there and don't get stressed!

APRIL 3

~Day 94~

Reset

I woke up at one o'clock in the morning and could not go back to sleep. I listened for forty-five minutes to my rain app. I listened for forty-five minutes to a story on my Audible app. I listened forever to NPR broadcasting and finally got up at 6:00 a.m. exhausted. I don't know what woke me, but no matter what I tried to do, I could not return to the wonderland of dreams. I said to myself, "Self, this is going to be a long, long, day." I have class in the evening, and I am going to be exhausted. I don't usually take naps because it disrupts the sleep patterns of a person. I am going to take some time to rest, to restore, and reset. Perhaps, you need to reset your day today! If you do, take a moment and reset.

APRIL 4

~Day 95~

Official Weight Day

I woke up this morning feeling and sensing that today would be a better day than yesterday. I did not feel exhausted or racing in my spirit. Wednesday is my "official" weigh- in day. I have weighed in on Wednesdays for nearly five years. I have two scales in my bathroom. What is wrong with me? I will have to examine the reasoning behind having two scales in a different Daily Window entry.

I had gained two more pounds in three days. I looked down and said to myself, "I am not changing my attitude today over this craziness. I am still feeling a sense of peace today." Another time, these two pounds would have sent me spacing, racing, and being aggravated. Don't allow anything to darken your beautiful day. Don't allow strongholds to keep you down. I am learning that the scale is a stronghold for me. I am going to battle this craziness, and I already know who will eventually have the upper hand. Remember, keep the peace in your inner soul. Don't allow work, people, or scales get you down today, even if it happens to be some type of official weigh-in day.

APRIL 5

~Day 96~

Hold On

I looked out my office window this morning, and what did I see? I saw a beautiful blue sky. I looked again, and I saw trees moving back and forth. The wind was blowing violently. I said to myself, *Old Man Winter is still here.* Both the calendar and the weather people say it is supposed to be spring weather. Not true yet. I looked out again and saw the trees trying to stay upright, but the north wind was relentless. The trees were trying to hold on. Fifty years ago, when I looked out of my window, all I saw was despair. Martin Luther King had been assassinated. People were in shock, and riots took place right outside of my kitchen window. We had to hold on in those difficult times. We have to hold on in the midst of troubles, heartaches, disappointments, mistakes, and doubt. In order to right a wrong, many times you have to just hold on. The winds of injustice may try to hold you back, but you must press on; you must hold on with the help of our Lord and Savior. He will hold you up and guide you in all things. Change will come. Trust and obey in His teachings.

APRIL 6

~Day 97~

Words Matter

As I look out my window, I think about my father. Interesting that I would be thinking about him today. I think about some of the conversations that we held. I don't think he was skilled or capable of having a positive conversation with any of his five children. It was not in his communication toolbox. Don't get me wrong; I do believe in his own way that he loved us. He simply did not know how to say it or show it properly. Words matter. No excuses. Words matter.

    I knew that he trusted me with his life. He would not have surgeries until the doctors had spoken to me first. I didn't know that my father talked to other people about us until I met one of his coworkers. He told me that my father was very proud of all of our accomplishments. He shared that my father talked about us all the time. I was shocked. This conversation told me something about significant about life and my father. Words matter. It would have been wonderful if my father had shared those words directly with us children. We must be careful with our words and how we use them. Words matter, so use them wisely today.

APRIL 7

~Day 98~

New

When I woke up this morning, I dreamed that I was pregnant. I laughed at myself, as you are probably laughing right now. You, pregnant at ninety! What a joke. A real nightmare. But you know something? It's not such a crazy idea. Samson's mother in the Bible was old; so was Sarah, Abraham's wife, and let's not forget Elizabeth, John the Baptist's mom. But I don't think my dream was about me with pregnant with a child but rather pregnant with an idea. Being pregnant is about giving birth to something new. Something that has never been here before. Maybe you are birthing something new. Allow God to direct you. Don't be afraid to get out of your comfort zone. God has a new plan for you. Trust Him.

APRIL 8

~Day 99~

Different

When I was probably five or six years old, I knew I had to make a choice. I had to decide whether or not I would serve God or choose to serve the world. I knew that I needed to dedicate my life totally to serving God. I know that God was calling me to serve *Him* wholeheartedly. I didn't know totally what that meant at the time. I was different. Are you different? I knew intuitively that I would have true joy if I followed the path of righteous. I knew that I needed to listen to His still voice when He spoke to me. Sometimes, people that you know and love will think that you have "five heads" when you make a choice. I knew instinctually that I had to serve God. I knew that I was different. People will not always understand your walk on this earth. Remember that. You are different. We want to be known as authentic servants of the Highest God! I believe that believers are being called to be different (a peculiar people). Authentic people. Real people. People who totally trust in God. No play acting.

APRIL 9

~Day 100~

Conscious Mind

I have been spent some time thinking about the conscious mind. The mind is amazing. We serve a God who is amazing! A God who gave us each an amazing, conscious mind. Just think about that. We can be sitting in a room full of people, but our minds are actually three thousand miles away, in Aruba or Spain. Amazing. It is important to feed your conscious mind with good, positive soul food. Think about what you think about. Let's ensure that we get a daily dose of positive thinking in our heads. Don't focus on the negative, but rather generate a positive stream of good thoughts. Society wants nothing better than for you to be down on yourself. Stay focused, stay positive, and be beware of all the good that is out there.

APRIL 10

~Day 101~

Due Time

I woke up this morning with a smile on my face. Today is Tuesday. We have early morning prayer at the church on Tuesdays. I have always loved going to church early in the morning and praying with my brothers and sisters of faith. I love the quietness and stillness of the building and the people. It is a beautiful experience to be in a community of believers, who love to cry out to God about their children, the nation, jobs, relationship, and marriages. It is great to be with like-minded people who believe in the power of prayer. People who come to church, expecting something great to happen when they cry out to God. The results of those prayers could be amazing miracles, or they could be as small as an uplifted soul. Check out Psalm 27:14.

APRIL 11

~Day 102~

Do Not Lose Faith

People are losing faith in prayer and the power of prayer. Don't. Don't lose your faith in the power of God. Don't lose your faith in believing that God doesn't hear your prayers. He hears and He is patient with us. He will answer in "due time." The only thing is that His due time is different sometimes than our due time. A sure sign of maturity in the faith is when God is silent about what you should do next. You pray and you don't get an answer. The answer is keep praying, watching, and waiting in obedience to *Him*. I know this experience very well because I continue to sit and wait for my next assignment. I continue to go about my business of praying, crying out to God, and being faithful to the routines of worshipping Him. The routine is being faithful to our Heavenly Father and waiting in anticipation of whatever He has in store for you. Do not lose faith.

APRIL 12

~Day 103~

Knowing

I woke up this morning knowing something very important in my soul. You know what that something important was? It was knowing that I was loved. It is a priceless feeling deep down in the heart of your soul. I know that there are millions and millions of people who do not know or have never experienced the joy of love. No matter what may be going on in your life at this moment, I want you to take a moment in time, to stop and say within your inner soul that you know that you are loved. This moment in time…it is a priceless moment that should stay with you.

You were loved before your essence was formed in the womb. You don't have a self-esteem problem because deep down, you know that you are loved. The value of knowing you are loved is priceless. You need to walk in the "knowing" of this love. You need to walk today, and every day in the knowledge, of the knowing. Because the "knowing" of our love helps to brighten the look of today and the promise of tomorrow.

APRIL 13

~Day 104~

Cold

I woke up this morning with a terrible sore throat. I felt awful. I am going to take my own advice and rest today. My throat hurt and I could not swallow. I said to myself, Am I getting pneumonia again? My chest was feeling a little heavy. I am going to rest today and get my strength back. I believe the saying is "feed a cold." I am going to try to eat some oatmeal and rest. It is very important to take care of the soul, mind, heart, and body. Today, I will take care of the body. May you go and do likewise. Love and take care of yourself. Catch the first signs of something happening to your body, and you may avoid the severity of the next level of sickness.

APRIL 14

~Day 105~

Heavenly Zip Code

I went to a funeral today. I would have to say it was more of a homegoing. It was a service with some crying but more rejoicing and laughter of a life lived in Christ. Everyone who was a believer in Jesus Christ knew the new zip code and address of the dearly departed. Jesus said in the gospel of John in the New International Bible in Chapter eleven, it says, "I am the resurrection and the life. The one who believes in me will live, even though they die; and whoever lives, by believing in me will never die." Do you believe this statement? I believe it. I no longer fear the unknown of death. I do less hurrying and worrying. If I am going to teach you any extra "stuff" this year through these writings, it is to do less worrying, fretting, and hurrying about things. Fix your heart and mind and soul on the things of the spirit. Fix your heart and mind on the new heaven and earth, and what that means within your soul. Enjoy the beauty of this day because it will never come again. Trust me, I know.

APRIL 15

~Day 106~

Tax Day

I remember when I was a kid, my parents would get tax refund check. It was a little like Christmas around our home for one day. We would get a few extra things for the house. We would go and purchase special sandwiches and have ice cream. It was a great treat. I remember that my parents always filed their taxes on the last day. They never had enough money to file their taxes right away. I guess that is why I like to file my tax returns right away. Today is the last day to file on time. I will always be thankful for Tax Day because I knew at some point, our family unit would have one less difficult day. Trust God. He will be with you in all things.

APRIL 16

~Day 107~

Raining

It is raining outside. When it rains no drops are the same size or shape. What a miracle! Enjoy the life-giving fruits of the rain, and don't hurry to get out of its way. Worry and hurry are the twins that can steal or rob your health. Don't allow anything to rob and steal your physical or spiritual health. We are only on this earth for a season of time, so enjoy it and try not be so stressed. Listen, hold on to this day because it will never come again. This day is precious because you know what? It's the only day that we have right now. This day is a gift from God, so we need to receive the gift in the right mind, heart, and spirit! Don't hurry through it, but rather enjoy the essence of the moment.

APRIL 17

~Day 108~

Routine

Every day, we do what we call routine, which means doing the same ordinary things in our lives every day. Every day, we wake up and brush our teeth (I hope) and wash our faces. Every day, we wake up and go to the sink and just turn on our water. We take these things for granted because they are all considered routine to you and me. Every day, we wake up and we just get up out of bed. Routine. What if we did not have this routine? What if we woke up this morning and did not have water to drink or water to bathe in? What if we woke up this morning and we did not have a warm coat or heat? What if we woke up this morning and had no food to eat, or a place to call home? What if? Let's you and I be more thankful today, and every day, for the routines of life. Go and be grateful today for everything.

APRIL 18

~Day 109~

Do-Over

Sometimes, we need to a "do-over" in some certain areas of our lives. It's okay to do that. We need to give ourselves the opportunity to reset, "do over," or reboot. I don't know how your day started, or how it will end, but if you need to do a reboot, or a do-over, here is a free "do-over card." Use it anytime within the next ninety-six hours, if need be. Sometimes, we just need to restart. Enjoy the day because this day is both unique and special. You know why? This day will never come back again. Hang in there.

APRIL 19

~Day 110~

Today

God allowed each of us to cross over into today. If you did not start off well this morning, then use the "do-over card" I gave you yesterday! It is still good for today and tomorrow. Remember to praise God. Be thankful and love the people that are around you. Love the people who pray for you! Care for the people who care for you. Don't disrespect or verbally abuse people who care for you. Just love them. You have been allowed to cross over into a new today. Don't waste this opportunity! Walk in the light and the Source that has been given to you today! Receive the message today!

APRIL 20

~Day 111~

Now

I took some cold medicine last night, and it made me tired. Have you ever done that? How did it make you feel? I am dragging today, and that is the reason I don't like taking medicine. I have a busy day ahead of me. I have to meet someone for a counseling session, and I have to attend a funeral. I am right in the middle of right now. You know what? I am going to take some of my own advice. I am going to take a chill pill. I will not allow the "nows" of the world dictate my mood or actions for the day. The day is beautiful, and I will walk in the beauty of the day! What about you?

APRIL 21

~Day 112~

Checking In

I went to the gym for the first time is in several days. It felt really great to be in the gym. It felt good to sweat. It was like a going back to something familiar. I totally enjoyed my experience at the gym. I was out of step, but it was okay. I did not realize how much I missed it. I pray that I continue to feel better each day, so I can get back to my regular schedule. It is good to check in on your experiences and some of the things that you have not done in a while. How about checking in with your Heavenly Father? Just a thought.

APRIL 22

~Day 113~

Lessons

I love to preach. I love to share the word of God with folks. One day, you never know—God may call you to preach or teach. It is an amazing thing when you actually see folks learn from the lessons of the word. The light goes on in both their eyes and their minds. One of the best moments in life is to experience the lessons of life from the word of God. Open up the word, and learn a new lesson today.

APRIL 23

~Day 114~

Keep at It

You have to work at relationships that are important to you. You have to "keep at it" every day. No one can read your mind. No one on this earth truly knows what you are thinking. The only one who knows is Jesus Christ. The rest of us have to work at communicating in the best fashion possible. We have to learn not to take each other for granted. You have to "keep at it" when building and creating trust, love, and understanding. You have to "keep at it" within your relationship with your significant other or soul mate, because it only grows with nourishment. The nourishment is love, respect, kindness, gentleness of tone, volume, rate, and understanding. Keep working at it.

APRIL 24

~Day 115~

Special

As I shared with you in another Daily Window, I love Tuesday mornings. Early morning prayer time centers me for the rest of the week. My body wakes up all by itself on Tuesdays. It is as if the spirit in my body says, "It's time to get up and go to meet with God and with some of His special people." I love to hear my friends pray. It is wonderful to hear Louise pray. She is ninety-two years old. She normally sleeps late except on Tuesday mornings. She automatically wakes up and walks to the church and prays for everyone who comes to mind. I pray that if I reach ninety-two years of age, I have all my faculties and wits about myself. I want to be able to walk, talk, and pray. Praise God for His many mercies and much grace. Enjoy the day. Isn't that special?

APRIL 25

~Day 116~

Space and Grace

Time is precious. I am learning to value it more. In learning that time is precious, I am learning about space. Some folks need more time to process. I am learning that by waiting to discuss some issues, you get a better response. In my gym class today, I felt that my gym buddies needed some space. Maybe because the day was rainy, but no one wanted to share in class. The class is usually very chatty. The class was quiet today. I don't know what problems they each had on their minds and hearts. As you go through your day, maybe people are quiet or responding differently; give them space and grace. Don't assume they are upset with you or have a problem with you. They may just need some space and some grace.

APRIL 26

~Day 117~

Worry

I hear the birds singing from my office window this morning. As I was reading my scriptures this morning, the subject was worry. It says that we cannot add an hour to our lives, "so why worry about so many things?" The illustration used in the Bible was about how the birds are taken care of by God. We are far more important than birds. I wished that I had understood the principle of not worrying when I was a kid living in the projects. I can remember my mother being so upset about issues of life. My mom was so worried about bills and so forth. Looking back and reflecting on her pain, she probably had an ulcer before she had cancer. Practice your faith in not worrying about the things of this world. Life passes too quickly. Enjoy today.

APRIL 27

~Day 118~

Worry-Part II

I have a confession to make. I was worried about an outfit that I was going wear at a social event. How silly can it get? True confessions. I knew that I should not have been thinking about something as insignificant as that. But to be very honest with you, I was thinking that I would look like the Goodyear Blimp. I had gained twenty pounds. I was worried. What really helped me process this concern was a word from the Good Book. If God takes cares of the birds and they don't have to worry, it says in that same passage, not to worry about the clothing that you wear. Those words hit me like a ton of bricks. I received the message from the Lord. I needed to let go and allow God to continue to move in my life. Just a thought. Don't allow your "own personal stuff" cause you to worry and fret. Enjoy today, because tomorrow is not owned by anyone. You can't claim it because it has not been given to you yet!

APRIL 28

~Day 119~

Beautiful

When I am processing about writing the Daily Window, I am flooded in my mind with many subjects. But I must remain true to the overarching philosophy of the Daily Window. I must speak the truth shown to me at the actual time that I sit down to write it. These moments are precious moments to be captured in their essence. Spend some time today seeking to know what God would have you to with your life today. Are you on the right track? Are you listening to His Voice? Beautiful. Be thankful to our Lord and Savior for giving us a second chance. Beautiful. Enjoy your day today.

APRIL 29

~Day 120~

The Month

Where did the month of April go? We are approaching the end of April! Do you remember what has happened in the month? We moved through it so quickly. As I process the last three weeks, I asked myself several questions. Did I experience joy throughout this month? Did I live life to the fullest doing these cold days of April? Do I have any regrets? Did I create any new regrets? What struggles have I been able to overcome? I ask myself, Am I growing as a believer in Jesus Christ? What has been my relationship with my Lord and Savior? How much have I been in communication with Him? I am learning that the only true way that life can truly be experienced is to have a real, authentic relationship with God. It has to be real. The relationship has to be real. The only way to grow in any type of experience is to be honest and real. Put Jesus first and everything else will fall into place.

APRIL 30

~Day 121~

Woke

How did you wake up this morning? In a poor or good state of mind? It is important to know and remember how you first woke up because it sets the stage for the rest of your day. I woke up with a song in my heart. I woke up thanking God for memories of yesterday. You know, there are so many things that can trip us up from having a great day. The worries of life can rob us of the beauty of the moment and the opportunity to enjoy the last day of April. Remember, that this day is precious and don't allow any individual's fleas to cause you to have a bad day. Even as I look out my window and see an overcast sky and rain falling, I remember how I woke this morning with memories of yesterday and the thought of future memories. It is well with my soul today. We can only respond to today because today is all that we have. Remember, we do not own time. Time keeps its own time. You have to take care of these moments and remember how you woke this morning. In a home that was not cold and had running water, food in the kitchen, and an indoor toilet. Remember that you are blessed and highly favored.

MAY 1

~Day 122~

New Beginnings

Truth sharing time today. Total transparency. The month of May is one of the months on the calendar that has many new beginnings for me. I remember in May that I recommitted my life to Christ. Prior to this time in May, I was just playing at church. I would go to church, if it was convenient to my time, my purpose, and my schedule. I would pray to God, read my Bible as a chore, and play at church. I recommitted my life totally to Christ and started a new life in Him. I have to be honest; it was tough in the beginning. To give up old habits, in body and mind, all at once was a hard thing to do, but the Lord told me that He would walk with me all the way. A new life of radical obedience to Him. I gave up the "stinking thinking" of my mind. Amazing grace. Amazing love. Talk to God about new beginnings in your life.

MAY 2

~Day 123~

In the Light of Day

Everything can be viewed better in the light of day. I mean everything: relationships, marriages, jobs, people, and new beginnings. You control what goes on in your mind. Don't allow the devil to use your mind as a garbage dump or garbage bag. Think about it and get control of what swirl around in your head. In the light of day, choose your thoughts and control the negative thought patterns. Develop a more positive spin on live and issues. Remember, you have a choice to be positive. You have to choose to be negative.

MAY 3

~Day 124~

Praise

This is the day that the Lord has made! We will rejoice and be glad. I woke up this morning, and I looked out my window, and I heard the sounds of life. The birds were talking, and the squirrels were gathering food. I believe they were praising God for another beautiful anointed day in Him. Thank God, I have not heard the woodpecker yet! He was here last week. He was letting everyone know that he was in the house. I just want to praise God today and thank Him for the warm weather. Don't you? My body just soaked in the sun rays of life and was saying, "Thank you, Father, for the sun." Praise the Lord for all of His mercies, goodness, grace, and the beauty of nature today. Look around you and see the wonder of God. Listen to the sounds of nature and praise God.

MAY 4

~Day 125~

Love Action

Amazing grace! God has allowed each of us to cross over into another new day! Take a moment to thank Him for allowing you to wake up this morning. Thank Him, even if you are tired, sick, disappointed, happy, or sad. It is important to start the day with thanking our Heavenly Father. Remember, worry and hurry are the twins that can steal your health. Don't allow simply things to annoy you today. Extend grace to everyone, including yourself. We can all use a little grace today—what about you?

Remember, there are very few things that really need to be done today. Remember when love is extended to you accept that love. It is in the actions of love that we know that folks care and love us. People don't have to buy you a diamond ring or a fur coat. I am talking about the little "expressions" of life. The unexpected cup of coffee or tea that is made just for you, just because they thought you would like it that way. Just the simple, small things of life. A love action is saying that I prayed for you this morning. I was thinking about you. Prayer is a love action, and we need more of it in our relationships today.

MAY 5

~Day 126~

Trouble

Let me tell you, no one is exempt from trouble. Trouble will comes knocking at your door when you least expect it. All of a sudden, issues happen and trouble appears. Problems will come your way. Trouble knows your zip code. As I look out my window and see people running down the street on this beautiful day, I want to tell you not to allow yourself to get depressed or in despair. Things will happen that you don't like. Situations will come that you can't fix with a text, email, tweet, or phone call. You have to walk in the understanding that you will sometimes face difficult days. I want to share with you today something that I learned early in my Christian life. God will never leave you or abandoned you in good or bad times. God shared with me in His teachings that He would not never abandon us or forsake us. Trust God and He will be there standing in the gap for you.

MAY 6

~Day 127~

Expectancy

Expectancy. Have we become too comfortable with ourselves and think that we can treat people any old way? Talk to each other any old way? Expectancy. What do we expect? Everyone is supposed to be treated with respect. Expectancy. True expectancy is when we look with anticipated hope that Jesus Christ will return soon. Expectancy is saying within our internal souls that we look to the future of a brighter day. We do not own the time of day, but we have expectancy that we will treat others with respect. Expectancy is this moment in time. Treat everyone with the expectancy of anticipated love.

MAY 7

~Day 128~

Soul Anniversary

Today is an extremely important personal anniversary for me. It was the day that I recommitted my heart and soul to Jesus Christ. I was lost. I was lukewarm in my faith and my commitment to God. I had become too focused on my "job." I had moved God out of first place in my heart and soul. I roleplayed at church. But God knew my inner soul.

I was struggling badly. It was a May day just like today. I said yes to God. I heard His voice within my soul and mind. You might wonder, "How does she hear Him?" I started to hear by reading and learning His holy word. I started to take my devotional time seriously. I started to make God a high priority in my life. I started to put Him ahead of everything in my life. I started to believe and live the commandments. To love the Lord my God with all my heart, mind, soul, body, and strength, and to love my neighbors as myself. I started to hear God when I cried out to Him. Psalm 16:7–8: Check it out.

MAY 8

~Day 129~

Refuse

Refuse to give up! Refuse to settle for just any old thing in life. Refuse to be disregarded. Refuse to allow anyone or anything to disrespect you. Refuse to be content in your devotional life. Continue to seek new levels of maturity in your spiritual growth. Satan wants you to be happy, content, and satisfied right where you are today in your Bible reading. He wants you to stay on the same page. He wants you not to finish the last chapter of the book. He wants you struck in your same "old stinky thinking." Don't allow Satan to get away with that kind of stuff. Refuse. Stop some of the busy things you are doing and ponder on Jesus. Refuse to give up peace of mind. Refuse to give up the calmness that can be in your soul. Refuse to settle for any old thing. Refuse to become stressed with the cares of the world. Jesus said in the Gospel of John, if we will follow Him all the days of our lives, He will be with us throughout the journey. Refuse to become complacent. Renew in Christ today.

MAY 9

~Day 130~

Preparation

I would like to share with you an important life tip. It is important to be prepared for both small and big things in life. You might wonder what goes into the two categories of big or small. You determine what is big or small for you. I watch the squirrels that live in my trees, and I see that they are always preparing for both small and big. The squirrels are living preparation every day. Read your word daily. Stay in faith. Keep the living word of God in your mind, heart, and soul. Prepare for the final chapter. Hang in there today!

MAY 10

~Day 131~

Encouragement

Be an encouragement to someone today. Remember, we can't allow the dark clouds of our minds to stop us from being a blessing to someone today. We were put on this earth to be in fellowship with folks. Be encouraged today because you are special. Tell someone today that they are special today. The true essence of encouragement comes from the True Encourager, our Lord and Savior, Jesus Christ. Be encouraged and be an encourager today.

MAY 11

~Day 132~

Airport Quietness

I have to say that it is really beautiful and quiet at two o'clock in the morning, especially at the airport. I had to take an early morning flight. There is beauty and stillness in the quietness of 2:00 a.m. The roads were empty and void of automobiles. No noise. No sound. So unusual. No horns. No angry and rushed drivers. Very thankful for the beauty of the day. The airport was quiet at that time in the morning. Few people were traveling that early in the morning. It was a great time to do morning devotions in the quietness before the noise of the day commenced.

MAY 12

~Day 133~

Just the Opposite

I am still amazed by how different people can be, even when they are raised in the same family. They can share the same experiences and be so different. I am on my way back from attending a wedding. I thought that this wedding would be similar to one that I attended with this family in the past. I have to be honest; I was dreading going because the other wedding was awful. Weddings are supposed to be inclusive and fun of warmth and love. The first wedding made you feel as though you were a burden. Neither the bride nor the groom ever spoke to anyone outside of their inner circle. The second wedding was just the opposite. Everything about the wedding was inclusive. I should not have prejudged this wedding. The influences of family are very complex. Change can happen. Don't prejudge situations.

MAY 13

~Day 134~

Total Love

I woke up this morning thinking about my mom. I am truly blessed to have such wonderful memories. I am blessed. I loved my mom with total love. She modeled unconditional love to her children. Do you know someone like that? Cherish them. Do you know something? I still miss my mom daily. She has been dead for over forty years, but who's counting? Model total love today. Jesus gave us total love.

MAY 14

~Day 135~

Very Complex Relationships

My mother's life was very complex. We could say that about all relationships. My mother was a special person in life. To me, at times she was bigger than life because of what she endured in this life. It took me a long, long time to process her life, and even longer her tragic death. My mother was ahead of her times. She worked while other women stayed home. I never asked her how she really felt about working outside with having small children at home. I do know that she did not like leaving us for as long as she did each day. We had no one to babysit us. My mom was gone for hours. She walked to work daily because she did not have funds for public transportation. Years ago, I followed the bus route that she walked daily. I measured the distance from our home; she walked for at least an hour and a half each way. My mom modeled love.

MAY 15

~Day 136~

More Anniversary Dates

When I woke up this morning, I thought that I was forgetting something or left something undone. I realized what today's date was and remembered. On this date, I would be running around my old school, getting all my facts, figures, and reviewing my presentation comments. This was the day that I met with the board of directors regarding the next year's school projections. This was always an extremely busy day. My body remembered what my mind forgot. Anniversary dates are important because they remind us of significant events that have shaped and can shape your life cycle. This was the day that we would determine how many teacher contracts would be extended for the next year. Powerful memories. Do you have some anniversary dates that are coming up?

MAY 16

~Day 137~

New Day

It took me a long time to learn the lesson of living in a "new day"—today. I had to learn not to borrow the troubles from tomorrow and not extend issues from yesterday. Today is new and it should be treated with respect and adventure. I spent far too much time thinking about the wrongs of yesterday and the potential ghosts of problems for tomorrow. I did not spend enough time in the moments of today. I wish I had been a quicker studier of life and enjoyed earlier moments of days. I am enjoying my new day today. I am learning to live in the moments of today and not allow the craziness of things, situations, and people, to enter my spirit. Take a moment to refocus, and remember you only have today. Breath in and out. Reset if you started your morning out tired, frustrated, angry, lonely, or disappointed. Remember, you only have this new day. Enjoy the adventure in Christ.

MAY 17

~Day 138~

Mist

I am so thankful and grateful to God for birthing within me the Daily Messages from my Window. Time moves on and unless we capture the moments, they disappear like a mist. Check out the book of James in chapter four and what he says about life being short like a mist. Enjoy today; the only time that you have is today. If someone is not treating you well, shake off the negativity, and move on with your day. If someone has said something to you harshly today, shake it off and move on with the course of your day. Don't allow anyone to take up or use your time with negative essence. Remember that today!

MAY 18

~Day 139~

Favor

Favor. Well, you do have favor. God has allowed you to wake up this morning and start a brand-new day. You get a do-over. Amazing. You get an opportunity to finish or start what you did not do yesterday. Aren't the possibilities exciting? I look out my window, and I see the beauty of the sky and the wind lightly blowing through the trees. I did not get an opportunity to quite capture that image in my mind yesterday. I see the squirrels playing in the trees. The adventure of the routine. Enjoy your adventure of the routine today. Remember you have favor, and you are blessed. Enjoy your new day and the adventure of the routine things of life. The seeing, the hearing, the watching, the listening, the studying, and the essence of being. Remember, you have favor; don't allow the frustrations of others impact your day of favor.

MAY 19

~Day 140~

Soul Care

Did you know that you have to do soul care every day? You have to take care of your soul. The soul is at the core of our lifeline. We have to feed our souls just as we feed our bodies and minds. You feed your mind with knowledge and understanding. You feel your body with good food. We need to feed our souls with heavenly food. Soul food. We need to read our holy word every day to self-care our souls. We must study the word of God just like Jesus did every day. He meditated on the word of God. We must seek to be like-minded. Soul care is an important survival essence in this life's journey. Please don't neglect your soul care, because if you do, you will not see the fullness of this life's adventure.

MAY 20

~Day 141~

Unfairness

Life is not always going to be fair to you. Looking from my window, I have witnessed a great deal of unfairness. I have observed unfairness in the lives of many people and have lived unfairness. Unfairness is something that comes upon all people. We say, "That's not right; that's not fair." True, many times life is not fair. Maybe you have been disrespected on your job by some unknowing or uncaring person. You didn't get the job title that you thought should have been yours. The person was unfair to you and didn't respect you. Let me tell you, that's their problem. Don't wear unfairness as a perfume. If you wear some perfumes too long, they begin to stink, and then they lose their purpose and power. Trust me, I know. Shake off other people's stuff, and walk in God's anointing on your life. Be free by not wearing the unfairness fragrance. The true essence of who we are is how we handle the unfairness and injustice that is thrown our way in life.

MAY 21

~Day 142~

Laugh at Yourself

As I look out my window, I am smiling. I am laughing about some silly thing that happened yesterday. You know, like entering a room and forgetting why you entered the room. I stop and think now that I am happy, I was able to remember that I had even entered! Today marks another anniversary: we have lived in this home for thirty-three years. I am smiling and laughing today because it is healthy for the mind, body, and soul to laugh. Try it. Don't be so serious. It is important not to dwell on so much negative stuff in life. The longer you dwell on issues, the disappointments, the negative, the greater the harm to you. I have seen so many people become what I label "the walking wounded," wearing everything that has been done to them. Too angry to engage in life. Content to be a victim and not a victor. Laugh at yourself, and be glad. We smile and laugh and say, "This is the day that the Lord has made, and we will rejoice and be glad in it!"

MAY 22

~Day 143~

Time and Seasons

The scriptures talk a great deal about time, change, and seasons. In the book of Ecclesiastes in chapter 3, it talks about timing and changes in everything. We are in a continual season of timing and change. As you walk through your day, value what is around you. Don't race through your day; rather, enjoy the experience and the moment of today. Change is coming. Recently, I was in the time to keep and the time to throw away season. I am glad that I went through this season because I now value everything around me. What time and season are you going through today? Read the book of Ecclesiastes, and see the wisdom of time and seasons. Life is so precious. You are highly favored and highly valued today and every day!

MAY 23

~Day 144~

Put on the Full Armor

Life can be difficult at times. We are all going to go through battles. We will have situations, disappointments, and illnesses thrown at us. Listen to me. No one is exempt from the battles of life. Faith people will battle with elements that are not necessarily flesh and blood. We who are people of faith will have to contend with different types of life's struggles. I never leave my home without first putting on the full armor of God. You would be wise to listen to this counsel and be prepared for the divisive struggles that will come your way. I love the breastplate of righteousness because many times, we think with our hearts first. When we put on the breastplate of righteousness, we are being protected within our hearts. Check out Ephesians chapter 6 in the Good Book.

MAY 24

~Day 145~

Put on the Full Armor—Part II

Today is a beautiful day. What a glorious day to be alive! As we walk on this planet, we are called as believers to walk in the truth. We must walk in truth and not continually enter into doors of stress. We must walk fully armed into doors of opportunity. You must be truthful to God, to your family, and to the friends who are around you. We must be truthful to the people we work with and equally to the people we meet on the streets of life. We must live in the truth of the spirit. The Lord teaches us daily the truth that we must walk in. God keeps us accountable to His commandments. I want to always walk in the truth of the Heavenly Father. Life is definitely less stressful if we walk in the truth of His holy word. Put on this piece of spiritual clothing every single day, and you will be a more joyful person as you walk.

MAY 25

~Day 146~

A Special, Rare Day

As I looked out my window, my mind floated back in time to thirty-eight years ago today. A special, rare day in my life was about to take place. A milestone of accomplishment. The weather was very similar to the way it is today. Nice, warm, beautiful, and alive. It was a special, rare day on May 25. We drove to the hospital after talking to the doctor. We were both in shock and suspense. We had never delivered a child before in our lives. We had never been parents before, and we were unsure of how to process all of this. We took classes and read every book on the universe, but we had never experienced a delivery. I was too stupid to be afraid. I did not take any form of medication at the hospital. A special, rare day. Our daughter entered this world. Amazing and still amazing. My world changed forever in that moment, and it would change again in two and a half years. I wonder if that is the way God feels every time one of us is born into this world. Amazing grace and love.

MAY 26

~Day 147~

After Contractions

No one told me about the "after contractions." My doctor didn't tell me, nor did I ever read about them in any books. An after contraction occurs when you still feel contractions after you have delivered the baby. You think you might have another child waiting to be delivered. Sometimes, the after contractions can be more intense than the original ones. Life is that way sometimes. You can be experiencing a crisis moment regarding a life event. You address the crisis, and you think that it has been taken care of and that everything is settled. You look around and something else pops up. Sometimes life will surprise you, and you will have some "after contractions" to address. I was just surprised. Be prepared and remember that when you go through a major, life-altering event, you might have some additional aftershocks. Good or bad, God has your back. Hang in there and be watchful in all situations.

MAY 27

~Day 148~

Your Calling

A calling is something that is God has ordained and that you were meant to do on this earth. How do we know it is a calling and not just a skill? A true calling is not about me; rather it is about advancing the gospel of Jesus Christ. We all have things that we do well at in life. There are skills that you do that might come very easy for you and difficult for other people. You could be good with numbers or great with words. You might sing like a bird or draw like a famous painter. To have these skills is great, but it might not be your calling in life. It has taken me a long time to walk into one of my callings in life. The calling of teaching. I have always known that I was good at conveying information about a topic and sharing that information with others. I know that it was a calling from God. You will know and learn your true calling. Ask God and He will guide you. Follow His directions for your life, and He will walk with you in freedom in that call.

MAY 28

~Day 149~

First Place

We need to remember that God seeks to be in the first place in our lives. We have many relationships and responsibilities. We need to remember who is to be in the first place in our hearts and souls. I was reminded yesterday by the Holy Spirit of what is most important in this life. God allowed me to walk the walk and talk the talk. Yesterday, when I started a new Sunday school class, it was God who gave me the words to speak. We sometimes forget in our accomplishments and schedules that it was God who made it a success for us. Remember who created you and protected you each and every day. The scriptures tell us that we are to love the Lord our God with all our heart, mind, soul, and body. We are to love Him wholeheartedly, and when we do that, everything will fall into place. Enjoy your day.

MAY 29

~Day 150~

Blessings

My mother never started the day off with a negative tone. Each day was a new day to her and a potential start for a new discovery in life. My mom was always trying something new. What a blessings and role modeling that was for me! My mom never carried over into the next day any of the negative junk from the day before. What a blessing to me! She was a great role model of strength in the midst of continual, ongoing craziness. She mirrored strength in the midst of all of her cancer battles, and she won the victory in my opinion. Nothing ever kept her down in life. She had a song in her heart, and she had Jesus in her soul. She modeled the love of Christ to me. I can only follow the examples that she gave me to give to you. How did you start your day?

MAY 30

~Day 151~

Be Stronger

Every day someone might give you a hard time or push your buttons. Yesterday, when I was at the doctor's office, a woman in the office gave me a hard time. She told me that I was wrong about the information that I had given her and basically that I did not know what I was talking about. She never allowed me time to truly finish my thought. I had just spoken to the customer service department and had been given the correct information. It has been a long time since someone has confronted me in this manner. As I got ready to say something like, "Could you please give me your supervisor's name?" Something stopped me. I believe it was the Holy Spirit. I believe the woman really wanted me to call her supervisor. I have taken the matter to prayer. All my friends say that I should call and tell the woman's boss. I'm not sure yet. I will pray on it further. I believe I am acting this way because I have the full armor of God on twenty-four seven. The Lord gives us the strength not to allow the craziness of individuals to get under our skin. Walk under His anointing.

MAY 31

~Day 152~

Tired

Sometimes, you just wake up tired. Have you ever felt that way before? You go to bed and you wake up more tired than when you went to bed. Sometimes, you will have days like that. Hopefully these types of days will be few and far between. This is one of my days that I am simply exhausted. I want to give you a piece of advice when you are in this state of tiredness. Take some time to rest. Take time to refresh and renew. When I am tired like I feel today, I know that my emotions are raw, cloudy, and misfiring on all levels. I plan to have limited contact so I can restore my mind, soul, body, and deep emotions. When we continue to work and respond to people tired and exhausted, we make serious mistakes, both in verbal and nonverbal communications.

    I was supposed to have a conference call today; I decided to postpone the call. You want to know why? This is an important lesson. I know within my soul that I will give better counsel tomorrow. I learned this lesson from the Master. Jesus took time to rest and restore Himself. We were not built to go continually in all activities. Take some time to renew, restore, and refresh. Try it and you will be better for it. Enjoy your day refreshed in the Lord.

JUNE 1

~Day 153~

Difference

Yesterday, I was down on the basement floor emotionally with negative thoughts. Today, I am rested in my soul, and all is well within my world. I see everything around me through a different lens. More hope, joy, and definitely with more grace toward the human race. Yesterday, I was tired of everything. Today is a different story. When you are rested, everything looks better. Trust me, I know. As I look out my window, I see an overcast sky with a threat of rain. In my refreshed soul, I see, spiritually and emotionally, an awesome and beautiful day with limitless possibilities. What a difference! What do you see when you look out of your window? Are you tired or refreshed on this beautiful day the first day of June? A day that holds a great deal of promise and hope? I pray that you are refreshed in the Lord on this very special day!

JUNE 2

~Day 154~

Aging Out

Whenever I go to my high school reunion board meeting, I am reminded of life and death. Every member on the board is at least twenty years to thirty years older than I. I am mindful of how slow things move as we age. As I look around the table, I could see that each board member was definitely aging. I look at myself and say, *if they are aging, my dear, so are you.* Time does not stop for me or anyone else in life. If they are aging, I must be also aging, and time does not stand still. I have always viewed these board meeting sessions as an opportunity for me to learn some critical life lessons. These ladies have taught me not to sweat the little things in life. I greatly appreciated their life lessons. Don't get frustrated or sweat the small things in life. Time does pass quickly. Be grateful for time and today.

JUNE 3

~Day 155

Fellowship

I was very excited when I woke up this morning. I was looking forward to fellowshipping with the new ladies in my class. I was wondering how many women would show up for the first session today. Most of the women invited did not run in the same circles with one another and didn't know each other. How many folks would show up? How many would be interested enough in the subject matter to change their weekly routine? Routines are hard to change. I am excited about the possibilities. You know what? A large number showed up for the first session. The subject matter for the first session was on grief and loss. I believe this topic was one that attracted many of them to come for the discussion. We have a common bond because every human being grieves some type of loss. This class has made my day. I left the class jumping and singing all the way home. We all need fellowship. Seek out a class or group today.

JUNE 4

~Day 156~

Sounds

I am listening to the raindrops as they fall on my window. The rain is coming down very hard outside my window. The sound of rain is very refreshing to my ears. I enjoy the sound of raindrops. The rain calms my nerves and gives me peace within my soul. Rain has always had this effect on me since I was a young child. I wonder what's up with that? I am not afraid of thunder. As a matter of fact, I rather enjoy the sounds of thunder accompanying rain showers. The rain is life giving to the birds, the squirrels, and all the wild animals. The rain is life giving to you and me. We need water in order to live. You can only go three days without water, and then you begin to experience serious side effects. We can live without food for weeks at a time, but not without the life-sustaining gift of rain. Find a sound that feels right for your mind. Take some comfort in it today. I plan on enjoying the rain. What about you?

JUNE 5

~Day 157~

Invite

I remember the first time that I was invited to church by someone. It was a big deal to me. Mrs. Saunders, our next-door neighbor, invited me to go to church with her. I don't remember anyone else in my family attending with us. I don't even remember anyone from her own household attending the services with us. A whole new world opened up to me by that invitation. I would have to say from the moment I entered the church, I fell in love with the people and the message. I found a new home. It was an exciting time in my life.

    I started to attend on Sunday morning, Sunday evening, Wednesday evening, and sometimes on Saturday. When I look back on family photos, I am missing from many of the shots. I was at church. Amazing what an invitation can do to your life! As I look out my window, I am extremely grateful today for that invitation. Mrs. Saunders did not know it, but God did; it was an invitation to a new direction, a new future, a new life in Christ. Be open to new adventures in Christ. You might be surprised by the direction. You never know where the journey might take you. Enjoy!

JUNE 6

~Day 158~

Invite-Part II

I take Zumba classes. I love Zumba. I have made new friends while I wait to get into the Zumba class. People ask me what I do for a living, and I tell them that I am a minister. They are surprised and interested in me. I plan on inviting some of my newfound friends to church. We talk a little about spiritual topics, and I don't think any of them have a church home. The Holy Spirit will guide, instruct, and tell me when to invite my new friends to church. I wait on the Lord. Invite some friends to church with you. I saw a poll once that said over 80 percent of the people will come to church if invited by a friend. Develop new friendships with people in different places.

JUNE 7

~Day 159~

Extremely Thankful

As I look out my window today and reflect back in time, I am struck by God's ever-gentle hand. I am extremely thankful for His presence in my life and for the people He has put in my life. I am still in awe of His greatness and that He would take the time with me. He is awesome! I am humbled and extremely grateful to Him for this wonderful life. I plan to look out my window and to continue to reflect on His goodness and mercy all the days of my life. Go and do likewise. Be thankful today.

JUNE 8

~Day 160~

No Time

I was on my way to the gym, and I could not stop smiling. I don't have time for craziness or negative feelings. I have no time for my mind to get twisted in some dark place. I have no time for my mind to second-guess the blessings that I have received. I have no time for my mind to put down the great things in my life by calling them "just okay." I am blessed and highly favored. My dear children, it is all about your outlook on life. Don't allow anyone to put their craziness on you. Don't allow your own inner self to put craziness on you. I am glowing and feel that anointing within my bones. New life growing and bubbling to come out. I am glowing. What about you?

JUNE 9

~Day 161~

The Anointing

I went to an awards dinner last night. A small intimate gathering of individuals. As I sat and chatted with one of the guests, he said to me, "I find you very easy to talk to. You really listen to people. I never share this much information with anyone. Have you always been like this? Do you believe in hope? What gives you hope?"

I shared with the young man that I had great hope in the future because I knew and believed in the final chapter of the living work of God. He knew what I was talking about on a spiritual level. He left church over twenty-some years ago when his mother died. She belonged to a church that did not believe in doctors or medicine. After the day she died, he never entered the church again. He asked me numerous questions. He asked me why I was so sure of my facts and beliefs. I told him that I believed in God and that I truly believe that He still speaks to us today. I told him that I have the faith to believe. I also was aware that this young man was drawn to me. It has happened before whenever I am around people who question whether or not God exists. They are drawn to the Holy Spirit who resides in me. They sense His presence and start to ask me questions. This young man talked to me the entire night. It is the anointing of God on me. I receive it and pray that I never lose it. How is your anointing today?

JUNE 10

~Day 162~

Heroes

There are few heroes left in the world. People disappoint us. As I look out my window today, we are so blessed to have a heavenly Hero: Jesus Christ. He is calling up our names to the Heavenly Father and interceding for us right now. It doesn't get any better than that! God is on His throne, and our Hero is talking about us right now. He is sending His angels to help us in all kinds of situations. Please walk in that understanding today and every day. Jesus is our Hero.

JUNE 11

~Day 163~

Routine

Today is a routine day. What a blessing to have a routine. I shared with you an earlier Daily Window that there is adventure in the routine things of life. As a family, we have just concluded a huge celebration. When one member of the family is recognized, we are all a part of that recognition. The celebration was indeed wonderful and a special time. We had a great time coming together as a family. Sweet times were shared over great food and great family conversations. New memories were formed and forged. Relationships were nurtured and enhanced. New friendships were developed and will be treasured. With all that being said, it is good to get back to the routine things of life. The daily essence of living. I am feeling very blessed to be able to have the time to reflect from my window. Most folks don't have time or have the desire to stop and listen. I sense and know the peace of stillness and quietness around me. It is wonderful. It is priceless. Seek the adventure in the routine things of life. The daily routine of seeking and knowing the love of God and serving *Him*. Check it out.

JUNE 12

~Day 164~

Waiting Room Again

I sometimes think that I have spent half my lifetime in a waiting room! Well, maybe that's a bit dramatic. In truthful reflection from my window, I would have to say quite a bit of time. I can't truly measure all the hours sitting in waiting rooms. I am currently in New York waiting to go into the waiting room with my sister. Memories begin to unfold from my memory bank of yesteryears of sitting in waiting rooms. I was always the one who took the other children to the hospital. We used the emergency room as our primary care physician. I would wait for hours for my siblings to come out of the treatment room. I would wait hours at the drugstore for the medicine to be filled. There was only one drugstore in our neighborhood to fill our drugs. The waiting room helped me to really learn how to pray, be focused, and look to our Savior for help.

JUNE 13

~Day 165~

Moments

Enjoy the moments of life. We move too quickly through these days. We say things too quickly. As I look out my window, I wished that I took more time to enjoy life's moments. We will never get these moments back ago. Time is truly fleeing. Trust me, I know. We can never take back what we said moments ago. Someone I knew recently shouted out some comments at a meeting. It only took a moment for him to yell during the meeting. He couldn't take back the words he shouted. Everyone looked at him in disbelief. I believe he wished that he could now take those comments back. If only he had controlled his impulses. If only he had taken a moment to think about the impact of his words. If only he had thought for a moment. Now, individuals are upset and planning to have a meeting with him regarding his "moment." Take some time to reflect and enjoy the moment before we speak.

JUNE 14

~Day 166~

Respect

In the scriptures, we see that Jesus got upset a few times. He did not respond negatively to insults hurtled at him personally. We saw Him get upset when the money lenders were trading in the church. He became upset when the Pharisees were taking and feeding off the misery of other people. Jesus spent the majority of his ministry time listening and fulfilling God's purpose. We would be wise to learn, listen, respect, and respond, with Him as our example of public discourse. As Jesus walked on this earth, He treated all people with respect and listened carefully to others' opinions. How will people know that we are different? They will know it in part by the way we conduct ourselves in our ability to listen to opposing points of view. Respect one another in love.

JUNE 15

~Day 167~

Casual

Casual is nice. Casual is comfortable. We live in a society where everything and anything is allowed. No restrictions or taboos. You can wear socks with heels. You can wear or not wear nylons to special occasions. You can wear any color, and there are no restrictions on clothing matches. When I was growing up, if you did not wear the proper nylon with your outfit, it was a social taboo. Today, you can wear anything you want to church. No problem here. When I was a kid, I searched for a church that would embrace me for who I was and not for how I looked. I have to tell you; it was a long search. I am thankful that I found a church that embraced the soul of the individual and not looks. I remember that I used to be very casual in my approach to my worship time. I am not saying that I don't approach my Lord and Savior on a personal level. He wants us to be in relationship with Him on a first-name basis. I am talking about my devotional approach to Him. I don't believe that we should take our relationship with Him for granted. Many times, when you open the door to casual, you get used to being casual and routine. May your worship time be special today with our Lord and Savior. Have a blessed day in the Lord.

JUNE 16

~Day 168~

Balance

We all need to have balance in our lives. We hear people say the word *balance*. What does it mean to you? What does it mean to me? Balance was a skill that I had to learn later in life. It is one that I am still trying to obtain. Balance is a state of being equal in behavior, emotions, attitude, and ways. Not getting carried away by some event or situation that takes us off course. I was always out of balance when I was a kid. I ate too much and did not exercise. When I did exercise, I went to extremes. I don't ever remember balance in my childhood. We either had too little or too much! Life needs balance.

As I grew into adulthood, I did not know balance. I worked too hard. When I left one company, they had to hire three additional individuals to fill my duties and responsibilities. It is a wonder that I did not die. It is only God's providence and grace that spared me. When I look out my window and remember those times, I needed balance in my life. I made so many mistakes. I am learning balance in all areas of my life. I pray that you learn balance in all things.

JUNE 17

~Day 169~

Dads

Dads come in all different shades and sizes. Dads come in all different types of personalities and spirits. Some dads are happy, and some dads are sad. On Father's Day I saw many dads in the restaurant where we celebrated. As I surveyed the room, there was one father who really stood out in the restaurant. He was there with his three daughters and his wife. The father was facing me in the restaurant. He was in my direct line of eye contact. I paid attention to him because he looked so sad and depressed. His wife was talking to him very calmly. The girls were sitting calming on either side of their dad, and he looked like he was getting ready to burst into tears. His face grew red, and he seemed as though he was fighting back the tears. Maybe he was thinking about his dad today. Whatever was happening to this dad, internally the grief was real. My heart bled for him. Some wounds are old. Some wounds are new. Honor your dad today and every day. Time can sometimes be very short.

JUNE 18

~Day 170~

Milestone Memories

Milestones are memories of taking a road trip with the ones you love and creating new memories. Milestones are things that we need to draw on when we look back on life's events. Milestones help us to plant and ground ourselves in today's reality. They help in developing our soul foundations of life. Walk in your milestone memories today. May the milestones that you develop be ones that are truly holy and wholesome. I look from my window, and I think about a thousand milestones that have made me and shaped me. I am deeply humbled and give praise to our Heavenly Father for giving me the opportunity to even make memory milestones. Go and make new memory milestones today.

JUNE 19

~Day 171~

Whatever

Do you ever use the word "whatever" in your conversations? It is a word that has many different meanings. You hear the word usage of "whatever" in many different contexts. You can never be sure of its meaning. I believe it is a very complex word. There are some words that people use that are clear and right to the point. No misunderstanding. The word "love" generates the message of love, either positive or negative. You know the difference. The word "home" sends a message for some folks of a sweet and safe place or a place that is dark and lonely. The message of the day is that communications can be tough to navigate. If you don't know the context of the message, there may be difficulties in the dialogue. The only way that we can truly convey the message and the meaning is to show our heart's message. When you communicate with people, share from your heart, and you will obtain better understanding.

JUNE 20

~Day 172~

Mad

We spend far too much time being mad. Half the time we really don't know what we are really mad about in the first place. When you find yourself in a place that you are emotional and your body chemistry has changed, give yourself a chill pill. Take a few minutes and say, "Is this worth any additional stress on my heart?" Don't get mad today about anything. You want to know why? You do not own this day. You are only allowed to be present for a moment in time. We get mad about things because we think that we are in control of everything. Looking out my window, I see that I spent far too much time being mad about stupid things in life. Let me bottom-line you: chill out and enjoy this beautiful day in the Lord. You don't own it, nor do you control it.

JUNE 21

~Day 173~

Summer

This is the first day of summer. I pray that it is a good day for you. Today is the longest day of the year. Amazing that we have all of this light in our day. How do you see yourself on this first day of summer? What is your image of yourself today, on the longest day of the year? Do you see yourself fresh, bright, old, young, disappointed, or excited? Only you know how you view yourself on this beautiful, bright summer day. On this beautiful summer day, how do you see yourself? I pray that you see yourself as beautiful, fresh, and ready to explore the world. I pray that you are more focused on keeping your soul fresh and restored in your spirit. I pray that this is a great day in the Lord for you. This first day of summer. As I look out my window, I hear the birds singing, and the squirrels are jumping. I see the promise of a great day. How do you see it today?

JUNE 22

~Day 174~

Smile

You woke up this morning to a brand-new day in Christ. God has spared you one more day! Smile. Celebrate this beautiful morning. Embrace your afternoon. Care for your evening. Don't waste the blessing of a new day by frowning about things in life. Smile. It takes a great deal of effort to frown. It really is not worth it. Smile. Be a blessing to someone on the street today. Your smile may make someone's day. They may have needed that encouragement to say that they were noticed or worth something to someone. Smile. You do not own the day. Since we do not own the day and we are only guest of this time, don't be so negative. Smile. Enjoy the day.

JUNE 23

~Day 175~

Sing

Sing today. We need to sing more. People don't sing enough. People are too busy yelling and fighting with one another about insignificant things. I was reminded of the need to sing when I heard a bird singing outside my window early this morning. The sun was not up, but the bird felt a need to sing. Initially, I was a little frustrated that the bird was singing before the sun came up. I said to myself, "What is wrong with that bird?" I have never heard a bird sing before daybreak. Maybe the bird just wanted to sing. Maybe she wanted to share her joy with the world. I liked that thought. I believe that the bird wanted me to hear her story today. I listened and smiled. We need to sing more. We need to listen to each other's song stories. This young bird wanted to share her story with me today. The bird may never be outside my window again. The song was beautiful. You have a song in your heart. Walk in that song today. Learn your song and share it with others today.

JUNE 24

~Day 176~

Personal Psalm

I believe everyone needs a personal psalm. In my Sunday school class, I shared with my group one of my personal psalms. My psalm is Psalm 145: "The Lord is trustworthy in all of His promises, and faithful in all that He does." This scripture has been a strength and a blessing to me. When I am low in spirit and I feel tense about things, I recite this scripture. I read and recite it every day. It is powerful for me. You need to find a psalm for yourself in times of peace and stress. When you have things going on in your life that could be hurtful, negative, and stressful, you need to have something strong to fall back on. Faith and scripture are two of the strongest substances. Find a guiding scripture that will sustain you in your time of need and want. Check out the psalms and enjoy.

JUNE 25

~Day 177~

Ask

Ask. Just ask. I have made mistakes a thousand times over because I did not ask. As I look out my window, the knowledge that I would like to impart to you today is to ask. What do I mean by the ask? I tried so hard to be in control of my own life and schedule. Do you know that was a very foolish mistake? I don't control life, nor do I really control my own schedule. God is in control of this world and life. His way is the better choice. He is amazing. He allows us the freedom of the choice. Trust me, I know of what I speak.

I now go to my Heavenly Father and ask Him, "If this is in your will and your way?" When I go to pray, I have learned to ask for instruction, guidance, help, discernment, and permission. I take a pause to listen to discern what my Lord and Savior is saying. His way is the better and more eternal way. Just ask.

JUNE 26

~Day 178~

Different Window

Today, I am looking out from a different windowsill. I am in a hospital in New York. What lessons will I learn today? What new stories will I learn in this great city? What new humanity will I see today? What new and interesting people will I meet? I just met a new surgical nurse who was very nice and helpful. As I look out this different window today, I see new things, new people, and new opportunities. As you go about life today, embrace it with awe and adventure. We should not allow the uncertainties of life to keep us down. We should embrace each day with freedom and excitement to learn more! Remember, don't allow bad news to keep you down. Don't allow rain clouds to rain on your parade today. Blessings as you may look through a different window on your journey today.

JUNE 27

~Day 179~

Sad

Today is not a day that I am jumping up and down. I am tired, and to be honest, I am experiencing sadness. There are all kinds of emotions in life, just are there are all types of people. We have mixed emotions, joyful emotions, excited emotions, and we have sad emotions. As I look out of my window this afternoon, I am sad. I am sad about several things in life. It is okay to stop for a moment in time and be sad. There are some things in life that we don't currently understand. There are some things in life that we would definitely love to change. We wish that we did not have to go through certain experiences. We wish that we did not have to go through difficult challenges. We wish that life was easier. It's okay to be sad. It is okay to pause, to grieve or reflect on what could have been. I know that joy is coming in due season. As it says in the scripture, "In the fullness of time." I believe that there will be great joy and excitement.

JUNE 28

~Day 180~

Rainy Day

The rain is coming down hard outside my window. I can hear the raindrops. It is very calming to hear the rain tap against my windowpanes. I feel very safe and warm inside my home. You know, every once in a while, it is good to stop and listen to the rain. By listening we slow down our pace. I think that slowing down our pace sometimes is a good thing to do. I am glad it is raining today. I needed to be slowed down in my activities. I had my whole day planned out with numerous activities. We all need to hit the pause button. Did you know that after the rain has gone, there is a fresh smell to the air? There is a newness about the moment of the day. I believe that I am just going to enjoy the rain today and put my checklist off for one more day. Enjoy and love your day in the Lord.

JUNE 29

~Day 181~

Fresh

I looked out my window this morning, and what did I see? I saw a fresh new day. A day that was bright, sunny, and brand new. I heard the birds, squirrels, and rabbits going about their natural order of things. I saw the sun and the blue sky. I looked up and I saw the wonder of God. I looked down and I saw the beauty of God. I looked around and I saw the hand of God. He has given us a fresh new day to start again, to begin again. Look at this day as a new beginning. Time has been reset. Time has been granted to each of us just for today. A new fresh day in the Lord. Don't waste the day thinking about what could have been! Think about the newness of each new day. New opportunities are coming. I feel it in the core of my bones. We have just been granted a new and fresh day in Him. I plan to get out in the world today and enjoy living the life that God has given me. What about you?

JUNE 30

~Day 182~

New Normal

Our God knows all about us. Our God knows all of our needs. Our God knows all of our sorrows, heartaches, troubles, and disappointments. He knows when we need or require a new normal. He is with us, doing all types of events in our lives. He is with us in the dark, sorrowful, and horrible times in this life. It says in the word that He will heal the wounded and the brokenhearted. I believe His word to be true. God healed me when I was lost, lonely, disappointed, brokenhearted, and abandoned. He created a new normal for me. When you have a life event that blows you out of the water and moves your earth, you need time to get back to a "new normal." Things will never be quite the way there were the day before the old normal. A new normal will appear at some point in time. How do I know this? As surely as the stars appear in the sky, I know that God is on His throne. He is with us always.

JULY 1

~Day 183~

Divine Dreams

Do you believe in divine dreams? Have you ever had a divine dream? These dreams are so powerful and cannot be forgotten. These dreams will continue to push forward into your conscious mind. Perhaps you should share your divine dream with someone you trust. Don't yell the dream out to everyone. Share the dream with someone you trust. People can shatter our dreams if we are not carefully. I remember reading in the scripture that God would come to people in the Bible and tell them things about the future. Divine dreams are power. God came to Joseph in dreams on numerous occasions in the book of Genesis and shared the future with him. He can and He will share divine dreams with you. Trust and obey.

JULY 2

~Day 184~

Hot

It is hot today! Some folks are crying about how hot the weather is today. It is summertime, and it is supposed to be hot. I like hot weather. No, let me make a correction—I *love* hot weather. I feel alive. I love to sweat. I feel alive. Winter is gone for the moment. No extra clothes are needed to keep you warm. No worry of falling down in the snow. Just feeling the breeze of warmth on your face. Think about the beauty of the summer and all the things that come alive during this season. Too many people only think about the heat of the day. I would say try to enjoy the beauty of the summer. Bottom line: enjoy any day that you receive as a gift from God. Walk in faith and grace today in whatever temperature.

JULY 3

~Day 185~

Tuesdays

My Tuesdays are filled with life, joy, peace, and great times of tranquility. Amazing grace. Amazing love. I love gathering to meet with the faithful of the church. I love praying for the needs of the congregation and for our country. We are in a time of uncertainty and unrest, and we need all the prayers we can muster. The saints gather together and cry out to God about the needs of family, friends, and strangers. We pray for peace, love, kindness, and the respect of mankind. At one time in my career—I have to be honest—I dreaded Tuesday mornings. I had a staff meeting that I had to attend on Tuesdays. These meetings served no real purpose and were boring. What a difference in my life now! I love Tuesdays and I love going to meetings with the saints. What a difference in my spirit! Find your "Tuesday morning" spot and replenish your souls.

JULY 4

~Day 186~

Freedom

My soul is free. There is a cost associated with the beauty and joy that I experience today. Our Lord and Savior, Jesus Christ, fought the good fight and paid the price. Freedom has a price. His death and resurrection set me free. I am free in body, soul, and spirit. I thank God for my freedom, and I pray for freedom of all people who are enslaved around the world. I pray right now for the people who are held in bondage and need to be set free. Furthermore, I pray that more people are set free in their souls by knowing Jesus Christ. Freedom. Debt paid. Free access to all.

JULY 5

~Day 187~

Unknown

Sometimes, the unexpected happens. We are unsure of our next step. We don't know. We are unsure. You know what? We are not supposed to know every next step. God is saying to you and me today, "I got you." God has said that so many times in the scriptures: "I got you." He said it to Abraham, Moses, Ruth, Elizabeth, David, Paul, and Mary and so many more. "I got you." He says it to you and me, no matter what is going on throughout our day: "I got you." We are not to be afraid of the unknowns of life. We are not to be afraid, fearful, or doubtful of what is to happen. God is with us.

JULY 6

~Day 188~

Overcast

Sometimes, our days will not always be shiny and bright. Sometimes, we have to go through a little overcast in our life journey. Overcast is anything that makes us feel darkened, gloomy, or displaced in our lives. I would have to say that for my first twenty-five years on this earth, I was in an overcast mode. My journey was dark, gloomy, and obscured by many things. I don't remember very many shiny days growing up. My days were darkened by sights and sounds of domestic violence in so many homes. My friends never talked about what went on in their homes. The city police and ambulances were steady visitors to apartments in my building. Some days, I could actually hear the punches through the walls. I could not wait to get away from that building and that way of life. I said to myself, "If I get away from all of this horror, I will never come back." You are going to have some overcast times in your lives. I promise you that these times will make you stronger. These times will cause you to rely more on God. I have learned to trust my Heavenly Father in all the shiny, bright, dark, gloomy, and overcast times.

JULY 7

~Day 189~

Surprises

A huge surprise happened yesterday as I sat in my office. My husband called out to me, and yelled, "There are goats in our backyard! Look outside in the backyard." I thought he was crazy. I went to our back deck, and there before my eyes were nine very large goats. The goats were eating the grass in my backyard. I could not believe that there were goats in our yard. I said to myself, "Go and get your phone to take a picture because no one is going to believe this story."

    I ran back to my office and picked up my phone. I ran back down to the porch and spoke to one of the goats. I said, "Hi, goat," and he charged at me. These goats are not like the ones that you see on television, all nice and friendly. My husband said that they tried to charge him in the driveway. Amazing. The animal control people came and led the goats back to their home. The goats lived on a farm close to our street. I learned that you never know who may visit you and give you a surprise. I also learned that just because we see something act nice on television, that does not mean it will happen in real life. Great lessons learned from my surprise encounter with goats.

JULY 8

~Day 190~

Get Back Up

Devastating things in life are going to happen. It is important that you know that some days on this earth will be filled with sorrow, despair, and disappointment. Every day will not be a party or a rose garden. You need to understand that there will be painful times in your life. As it says in the New International Bible, in Psalm 30:5b, "We may weep through the night, but at daybreak it will turn into shouts of ecstatic joy." Whatever, the challenges that are facing you at this moment, I say, "Get back up." You must get back up and move forward with your life. Don't allow the darkness of these moments keep you down. Get back up and move forward with the newness of life's opportunities. Don't allow the dark clouds to keep you from getting back to your starting point. Hold on to hope and faith during these times of darkness. Get back up and keep stepping forward today and every day.

JULY 9

~Day 191~

What's Up?

What's up with the way that we talk to each other? I have been pondering this question. We have all fallen short in our communications skills. In thinking about my communications with individuals, I need to do better. I have to do better. I will do better. You want to know why? I want "others" to be in my life. I don't want to be alone. I want to live a real life with people in my life. I have relatives in my family whom no one communicates with on a regular basis. You want to know why? It is because these relatives are not kind to people. Everyone in the family just got tired of the bad dialogue and decided to call it quits. I don't want to be one of "these people" that folks forget and sideline. I want folks to want to be around me and have me in their lives. What's up with your communications today? We all need to grow up in our talks with one another. Just a little food for thought.

JULY 10

~Day 192~

Waiting Room Again

I am back in the waiting room again. I guess I have more lessons to learn. As I enter the waiting room, I observe all types of people. Some of the people in the waiting room are very sick. You can see it written all over their faces, bodies, and families. The sick people are speaking quietly with their family members. Some of sick people are actually comforting the ones who are not sick. I see other sick people who are angry and want everyone to know that they are angry. I further observe some fearful people. They are afraid of what is going to happen next as they leave the waiting room. I see some folks who are confused and don't know what to do with the circumstance or situation. I observe some individuals who have hope in the waiting room. I observe, I watch, and I learn different facets of life waiting in the waiting room again.

JULY 11

~Day 193~

First?

As I reflect out my window this morning, I am reminded who is first in my life. It is important to have your priorities right from the start of the day. Who's on first in your life? Do you know who? What's first in your life? Do you know? What or whom do you think about first in the beginning of your day? What totally dominates your thinking? It took me a while, but I am thankful that I finally got it straight. I have learned to love the Lord my God with all my heart, mind, soul, and body, first. In loving God before all others, the rest of the priorities will naturally fall into line. You will love others better when you place Christ first. I know it to be true. I know that when I have been out of step with this order, my existence on this earth is dimmer. Put God first, and all the rest will come into order. I can testify to that knowledge and fact.

JULY 12

~Day 194~

Study and Practice

Yesterday in the Daily Window, I shared that in order to have a full life, God must have *first* place. How do you do this? I received an email from a follower asking a very critical question: "How do you put God first?" Great question. My response to that question is study and practice. You may think that to be odd, but it really isn't odd at all. Think for a moment of all the things that you are good at in life. You have to study and practice to be great. Am I correct? If you wanted to be a fitness professional, you have to study and practice. If you wanted to be a lawyer, you have to study and practice. If you want to be a teacher, baker, soldier, judge, runner, reporter, you have to study and practice. If you wanted to be a decent human being in this life, you need to study and practice. If you truly want God to be first in your life, you need to study and practice. Read your Bible daily. The Bible will help to center you in your thinking processes.

JULY 13

~Day 195~

Refocused

Every time I go on a trip, I am thankful because I get an opportunity to refocus. I am a creature of habit. I love the routine things of life. I love my office and the things in my office. I love where my computer sits, and I love where my desk is located. I love going out to my garage and getting into my car spot. I love doing my devotionals in my special place in the house. I love eating my cereal while I watch a favorite television program. I love routine. I love walking in my neighborhood up and down the same streets. When I take a trip, short or long, it breaks my routine. In breaking my routine, I am able to see a different viewpoint of life. Being away for a few days breaks our routine and allows us an opportunity to refocus.

JULY 14

~Day 196~

Exercise

I felt that I had a great workout today. I felt great taking Zumba. I love Zumba. It is the perfect exercise regimen for me. I am grateful that I found an exercise that is a great feeder for my soul. It is important that you find something that is going to keep you moving, both in your body and spirit. Get outside today and move your heart, mind, soul, and body in exercise. You will feel better for each step that you take.

JULY 15

~Day 197~

Remember

It is important to remember places, situations, and important facts. I remember this date because I had to present a very important report to my school's board regarding enrollment. I had to stake my abilities, skills, and reputation on what I presented. I remember that God was with me. God was with me as I traveled miles and miles to have my worked questioned and reviewed. The board of trustees felt that the school was now a burden. Many of the old board members who truly believed in the mission of the school had died. The new board members wanted to fund other projects. I remember that God walked ahead of me every step of the way. I remember, today on July 15, that God still walks with me and has my back. Remember, He will guide you in all things, and He will be with you. Remember.

JULY 16

~Day 198~

Yesterday

Yesterday was a glorious day! You want to know why? It was a glorious day because six individuals from our church declared their love for Jesus Christ. The six individuals were baptized with water and filled with the spirit of God. We conducted the baptismal outside in ninety-degree weather, which was probably similar to biblical times. Three children and three adults gave their testimonies just before they were baptized. The testimonies were well spoken and had heartfelt meaning to each message. Do you remember your special moment in time, when you declared before the crowd your commitment to God? Do you know that the angels were cheering you on that day? The angels were cheering you as they were cheering the folks yesterday. I think about John the Baptist and all the people that he baptized. It was the same yesterday as it was over two thousand years ago. We walk under the anointing of the same Holy Spirit. God is with us today, as He was with them yesterday. We walk under the amazing, incredible, and awesome anointing of His Spirit. Walk under that anointing, and remember the milestone of your amazing baptism today!

JULY 17

~Day 199~

Enough

I woke up this morning thinking about the word "enough." Do we ever get enough? What does that even mean, "enough"? I try not to make up meanings and definitions. I went to a good online dictionary that read, "Enough means never having to say you are sorry." No, that's not true. I was just checking to see if you are reading today's Daily Window. Daniel Webster's dictionary says that enough means, "adequate for the want or need; sufficient for the purpose or to satisfy desire." Do we have adequate for the wants and needs in our lives? Wow. I would have to say that I do.

I have far more than "adequate" in my life. I have far more than many wants in my life. I have more than is sufficient for the purpose of my desires. What about you? We have more than enough. We can go our kitchen sink and just turn on the faucet. We have more than enough water. We can go to the grocery store and walk down any aisle and chose from twenty different selections. We have more than enough. We can go to any automobile establishment and select from a hundred different cars. We have more than enough. Walk in the joy of enough today.

JULY 18

~Day 200~

Blessed

You are blessed. I love the song that goes, "Somebody prayed for me, had me on their mind, took the time, to pray for me. My mother prayed for me, my sister prayed for me, my father prayed for me." I took that song seriously. You are loved, blessed, and prayed for continually. You are blessed because you have been prayed for a million times already on this beautiful summer day. Do not walk in fear, shame, disappointment, angry, anxiety, or pressure of any kind. You are blessed and highly favored. God has already received a party line prayer for you this morning of protection, love, beauty, and joy. Enjoy your beautiful day.

JULY 19

~Day 201~

Hang in There

I look outside my window, and I see a beautiful day. I see a beautiful tree and a beautiful sky. It looks beautiful now, but that was not always the case. Some days have been dark, cloudy, and full of despair. I don't really know what kind of day you have been experiencing as you read this Daily Window. I tell you to hang in there because you are made from special stock. Your roots are deep, long, and attached to an eternal anchor. You may not "feel" it today, but that's okay. You don't have to feel the anchor. The anchor is always there. Hang in there! A new day is just around the corner. A new day is coming, and it will be waiting for you. Hang in there!

JULY 20

~Day 202~

Moods

What an interesting topic we are covering today in the Daily Window: moods. Every family has moody relatives. You might be moody. You work and live with moody people. Moody people exist in the world. Moody people exist in your world. You might be a moody person. We as human beings get moody at times. However, we do not have to allow other people's moods to change or alter our days. Think about it. Just because someone is in a bad mood, you don't have to modify your good mood. Think about it: you going along fine in your day until you come across your boss in the lunchroom. She is in a terrible mood. After your brief conversation with her, your mood has changed. Learn to navigate your moods better. Don't allow anyone to change or modify your mood.

JULY 21

~Day 203~

Keep Moving Forward

Change. Things happen. Every day is a new adventure. A shift in the way things are going. I want you to remember that you must keep moving forward. Life never stands still. Keep moving forward even if you experience a huge roadblock in your life's highway. I have experienced numerous roadblocks but didn't allow them to keep me from moving forward. If you are experiencing a huge life roadblock, get off your pity party and keep moving forward. You only have one opportunity to experience this beautiful planet. Shake off the fleas today, and keep moving forward with your life. Get out of your house, and keep moving forward. Lift up your mind on the beautiful things of life.

JULY 22

~Day 204~

Gift – Part II

Did you know that today is a gift? A gift to you and to me. Do you want to know why today is a gift to us? You and I don't own this day. We can't order up a day on our internet servers. We can't will a day into being. We are the recipients of this special day. God has allowed each of us to be a part of this newly created day. This day will never come back again. This day is unique. This day is one of a kind. What a gift! We are recipients of God's favor. We did not earn this extra day of life. The day was a gift to you and me. Please don't waste the gift that God has given you by being in a mood or angry. Don't waste this precious day by being sad or disappointed by some regret in life. Today is a gift. Walk, act, and appreciate what has been given to you free of charge. Thank God for the gift of today.

JULY 23

~Day 205~

Blessings

The Bible speaks a great deal about the blessings of God. God bestowed blessings on the people in the land. He bestows blessings on you and me every day. What does that mean? A blessing is "a favor or gift bestowed by God, thereby bringing happiness." Just take a moment, and think about all the blessings you have in your life. Think about all the blessings that God has bestowed upon you. I think about times when I was a child and my family did not have enough money to pay the rent on our apartment. Amazingly, God would show up and bless us with some funds to pay the rent. What a blessing! God's amazing favor. He gives us blessings every day. Take a moment today, and thank Him for some of His blessings. We will never remember all that He has bestowed on us. It is important to thank Him for all of His love. Just say, "Thank you, Father, for everything!"

JULY 24

~Day 206~

Opportunity

I got a wonderful opportunity today. I was able to go to attend a church service in the middle of the day. It was truly an awesome pleasure to attend the service. I love the way the minister of the gospel respected the holy scriptures. I love the way the members of the congregation respected the reading of the word of God. I loved the music that was played and the song leader who led the church in worship. I felt the presence of God throughout the brief service. The service was like a breath of fresh air. As I watched the congregation receive Communion, I saw people came from countries all around the world. Many different nationalities and cultures. The service reminded me of what it says in the scriptures: that people will come together from all nations. I am grateful that I got the opportunity to praise the Lord with saints from around the world! What about you?

JULY 25

~Day 207~

Summertime

We are in the middle of the deep days of summer. Hot. The days and the nights are hot. Some people hate the heat. I love the heat and the summer. What about you? Hot days make us slow down a bit. Today is a great day to slow and rest in the Lord! Enjoy this hot day of July and summertime. Rest in the Lord and give Him praise. Thank the Lord for the gift of today!

JULY 26

~Day 208~

Don't We?

It is important to communicate with honesty, love, and kindness. When we talk, speak, or share with one another, we need to be honest. Don't we? We want our love ones to speak "truth" to us. Don't we? When we share with our love ones, don't we want to speak with love and kindness? Don't we? We want open and honest dialogue. Don't we? To really communicate in life, we need to mutually impart thoughts and ideas that are in honest, love, and kindness. Don't we?

JULY 27

~Day 209~

Family History

I was talking with one of my sisters the other day, and we starting sharing about our childhood. We talked about our early family life with two parents and five children. Her memories of our early childhood days were totally different from my recollections. I happen to be ten years older than my sister, so I have a different context for our family history. We talked about family times and traditions. Family time was important. Contact one of your family members, and share your family history and traditions. Enjoy your relationships and your times together.

JULY 28

~Day 210~

Time Changes

Time changes. When I was thirteen years, I had an opportunity to babysit for the summer. I made only thirteen dollars a week. I took care of the child from seven in the morning until he went to bed. It was slave labor; I think as I reflect from my window. Time changes. Back during those days, people trusted other people with their children. Big mistake, even then. My father's boss was the one who set up the babysitting "opportunity." I was a slave working for his daughter. Maybe, my mother believed, it was better for me to be someplace else. The money I made helped the family. Times change. God watched over me and protected me. Time changes. Thank God for change.

JULY 29

~Day 211~

Memories

I remember when I was about twelve years old and I was caught in a blizzard with Mom. The snow and ice were unrelenting and kept coming down on us. We could not get a taxi or a bus. I will never forget that walk home with my younger siblings. No bus would stop. We walked miles and miles in the snow and ice. I remember trying to make it into an adventure for them, saying that we were on a mission. They actually bought that story for a little while. My sisters and I were exhausted. I imagine my mom was exhausted because she had already worked a full day's job. I remember she quit her job after that evening and did not work outside the home again. God sustained us that night, as He continues to do so this very day. Memories.

JULY 30

~Day 212~

Despair

We must move forward every day in hope and not despair. As I look through my window today and I see the trees moving, I remember my family going through extremely difficult times. My father's job had been on strike for months. The unions paid the workers limited funds. The families did not have enough money to feed their families. My father would go fishing to try to put food on the dinner table. I hated fish at that time. I hated the smell of fish. Fish was all that we saw during those days. Remember, I was only a young kid. My parents had no "rainy-day fund." They did not know what a rainy-day fund was with five children. There was always a need or emergency waiting to happen. We did not lie down in despair. We did not allow the evil one to rob us of our hope and joy. We always knew that God was on His throne. We still had hope and did not succumb to despair. Walk in hope, peace, and joy today. Forget about despair and lean on hope.

JULY 31

~Day 213~

Rise and Shine

I remember when I was a little girl; my mom would wake us children up with a song. She would wake us up gently from the night. Looking back on that time, it was a real blessing and gift. My mom did not yell or shout at us, but she gently spoke to us. She sang a quiet song of love. We need to be careful how we start to engage our day. We need to show and express our love to our families in verbal and nonverbal ways. How do you approach the ones you love? Perhaps it might be good to start with a song in your heart. Today, my song is "Rise and shine and give God the glory!"

AUGUST 1

~Day 214~

Again

Again. I find myself in the waiting room. What new lessons will I learn? Will we ever learn all the things we need to learn? I sit in the waiting room, waiting to hear results that might affect the direction of someone's very existence. Again, we sit waiting for the doctor to interpret the results of so many blood tests. We want him to tell us that everything is okay. We want to feel good again. Again, we wait. When I reflect on all the times, I have experienced in this waiting room journey, I know that my Lord and Savior has been right there with us. We walk under the anointing of the Holy Spirit! We wait in the peace of Jesus, knowing that He is also in the waiting room with us.

AUGUST 2

~Day 215~

Take a Moment

I woke up kind of tired this morning. My mind was saying, *take a moment and reset your body, spirit, and mind today*. You ever feel that way? Today, I am going to take a moment to regroup. I have just come back from a long car trip, and my body is saying to take a break. I am taking a moment. Sometimes, you need to take a moment to refocus or just listen to what your heart and mind are saying. I am listening to my body today and taking some time to just chill. Take a moment and listen to yourself. I guarantee you will feel better in all ways of life.

AUGUST 3

~Day 216~

Good Morning, Special Day

Good morning. Today is a special day. Do you want to know why? We have been allowed to wake up another day. Amazing! We have been allowed by our Heavenly Father to wake up and remember our memories. Good morning. We have been allowed to remember that this is a new day. I was at a church service last week, and I saw someone that I have known for many years. He did not remember me because of his memory loss. He was once a very active person. I am grateful for each day that the Lord gives us on this earth. I am grateful for memories on this special day. What about you? Thank God that you remember today.

AUGUST 4

~Day 217~

Birthday

My mother would make every birthday in our home special. Each birthdate of every sibling was significant in our house. No child was an exception to the rule. Every one celebrated and honored the special birthday. We did not have money for fancy gifts or even birthday cakes. We acknowledged the day with a special celebration of love. We gave the birthday person special grace passes. The birthday person did not have to do any chores for the day or week. Today is my sister's birthday. It is a special birthday for her. She received a new heart three years ago. My sister was sick for a long time, but she fought a great war. Because of her new heart, she celebrates two birthdays. She celebrates her original heart day when she was born. She also celebrates the day that she received her second heart—on New Year's Day. She feels really special and blessed. What special blessing do you have today?

AUGUST 5

~Day 218~

National Sisters' Day

As I was reflecting on my topic for today, someone said to me, "Hey did you know that today is National Sisters' Day?" Who knew? What does that even mean? National Sisters' Day? I don't really know, but the title did give me pause to think about my own sisters. I was blessed to have three sisters. As I reflect on my sisters, I think that you can't live with them, and you can't live without them. Due to the differences in our ages, I can remember the birth of my two younger sisters. I still remember when my mom brought my sister home for the first time. I thought to myself how small they looked. My two youngest siblings were only one year apart in age. Sisters are truly special. They know your funniest and darkest secrets. Sisters can help you change a horrible day into a day of sunshine. Do you have someone you call sister today? Give that person a call, and tell them how much you love them.

AUGUST 6

~Day 219~

Don't

Don't allow the craziness of another person's issues get on you today. Don't allow any person or any issue take away the sunshine of your day. You don't always have to defend yourself to other people. You don't always have to defend your principles or your personal ways. Walk in your assurances of life. Don't allow anyone to push your buttons or create a door of stress and uneasiness today. Remember the spirit in which you want to complete your day. Don't take on anyone's negativity, issues, problems, unpleasantness, or craziness. Chose to step out and block all of that craziness today and live a great day.

AUGUST 7

~Day 220~

Quiet Our Words

Sometimes, our words can create or cause irrevocable destruction and pain. Sometimes, we need to quiet our words and think of another way to express our opinions. The longer I am allowed to live on this earth, I become more aware of how we deeply hurt others with careless remarks. I think now of some of the words that I have spoken in truth, not caring how they strung. I wish that I could take back some conversations a thousand times. I wished I had learned the lesson of "quieting my words" just a little sooner. I think I would be a better person for it. Also, some people would not be carrying around my hard words. Today, before you speak, consider the tone and syntax of your messaging.

AUGUST 8

~Day 221~

Moments

Take a moment. Take a moment and think. Take a moment and appreciate that you have been given a moment. Take a moment right now and be thankful. Take a moment and be thankful for health care. Take a moment and be thankful that you had a bed to sleep on last night. Take a moment and be thankful that you have people who remember you and love you. Take a moment and thank God that He said He would love you always. Take a moment and think about today. God will always be with you. He will love you always. We have an amazing God. Take a moment and just say, "Thank you, God."

AUGUST 9

~Day 222~

History

My mother and I would sit in the window on the third floor of our apartment building, and I would continually ask her about life and family events. I grew up in that window and learned about my family roots. My father's mother was a teacher. I was amazed at that fact. At the time, when I was growing up in the city of Boston, I only experienced one black teacher up until tenth grade. To have a grandparent as a teacher was just an awesome fact. My mother told me that she also taught school for one year in the Deep South. I was shocked. I learned that my grandfather had a large farm, and he would supplement his income by working on the railroad. Take some time to learn your family history. You might be surprised by what you find out in life about yourself and your family.

AUGUST 10

~Day 223~

Unexpected

What is unexpected? It means "sudden, surprised, or unanticipated." You can get an unexpected compliment from someone you don't know, and it can make your day. You can be driving down the street and you get a flat tire. Unexpected. Life changes. What makes life beautiful is that each day has the opportunity to be different. Unexpected can lead you to make a new friend. Unexpected can completely change your course of direction. You could receive a notice in the mail that could unexpectedly change your life. Unexpectedly, I walked over a bridge one day in New York and just fell in love with the bridge. Unexpected. No day is really the same. Smile and be glad. Readjust your thinking, and you will see amazing and unexpected things in life.

AUGUST 11

~Day 224~

Rain

I woke up to the beautiful sounds of rain this morning. The rain was hitting my windows and air conditioner. I love rain. I love the beat and rhythm of the rain. I love the sounds and smell of rain. Rain seems to help center me in my core. God gives us rain. Water is life giving. We can live without food for weeks at a time. We can only go a few days without water. Rain is life giving. The farmers are always looking to the sky for the rain to come and water their thirsty crops. The firemen are always looking to the sky for the support of rain. What gives you calmness and peace of mind? It is important to find that extra sense of peace in your life. Seek God and walk in His comfort and peace today.

AUGUST 12

~Day 225~

Take a Moment

Take a moment and be thankful for the opportunity of reflection. Take a moment and be grateful that you can walk, talk, laugh, jump, and have freedom of expression. Take a moment and be grateful that you can read and write. Take a moment and truly praise God. Take a moment right now as you are reading this page, and thank God for the ability to read. I look out of my window this morning, and I listen to the beautiful sounds and wonders of life.

AUGUST 13

~Day 226~

Forgiveness

This Sunday, I will be preaching on the subject of forgiveness. What a tall order. Whenever you preach on a subject like being forgiven, you have to check your own heart. Is it clean? Have you gotten over the "stuff" that is trapped your own heart? There are many definitions for the word *forgiveness*. The definition that fits for me is "to cease to feel resentment against." To cease against what? I believe it is to forgive whatever traps our spirits from rejoicing in the Lord.

Unforgiveness blocks everything. Unforgiveness blocks growth and creativity. I am grateful and thankful to the Holy Spirit for continually showing me my areas of weakness. Sometimes, we carry things so long in our hearts that we think that feelings of offense or resentment are supposed to be there. Unforgiveness is like a cancer that breeds and takes away living cells. Is there someone you feel that you need to forgive today? Think about it and truly ask God to help you let it go!

AUGUST 14

~Day 227~

Early Morning Prayer

Jesus used to get up for early morning prayer. Amazing! I went to early morning prayers today. I wake up early to be ready for this special time in the Lord. I always enjoy going to church in the early hours of the morning to meet with other fellow saints. It feels very refreshing, and my soul gets uplifted in hearing the saints pray out loud. God is on His throne today. God is available with answers today. Take some quiet time today, and spend it with our Lord and Savior.

AUGUST 15

~Day 228~

Difficult Times

In life there will be difficult times on the journey. Not every day will be filled with song and dance. Not every day will be merry and full of joy. You will experience difficult times in this journey. Not every experience will be wonderful, but you will gain wisdom. No matter if you are going through a good, bad, or difficult time, I know someone who's got your back twenty-four seven. God is with you in and out of season. You want to see something amazing about God being with you? Check out Psalm 91, an amazing story of protection during the journey of life. I have experienced many difficult times in life. Check out the scripture, as it will help you during your difficult time.

AUGUST 16

~Day 229~

Stay in Your Own Lane

I was in a meeting the other day listening to a story about two friends. One woman shared that she wanted to support her friend. She wanted to give voice to the injustice of a particular situation. She admitted that she was wrong to jump into the middle of a personal domestic situation. She acknowledged to the group that as soon as she shouted an objection, she was clearly in the wrong. I asked her did she know that she had crossed the road and had moved into the wrong lane? She tried for a moment to justify the outburst but realized that no one in the room agreed with her approach to the situation. It is extremely important to stay in your own lane. You can't just say anything you want, whenever you want to say it. There are some lines, lanes, and boundaries that should never be crossed. My mom taught me early to really look at situations carefully and see what is below the surface. Check out fully what is happening in each situation. As each person is different, so are events and situations. Check yourself. Be sure that you are moving in your own lane and not someone else's today.

AUGUST 17

~Day 230~

Room Was Ready

Yesterday, one of the greatest singers on the planet passed from this life into the next one. In every situation and at every event, Aretha Franklin's voice has been a part of my life. Her music and lyrics voiced my emotions and moods. Her music expressed some of my joys, sorrows, or pain. She will be truly missed. I stayed up late into the night listening to her music. I was sad. I was sad until I saw a recent picture of her. You could tell from the picture that she was sick. She looked tired and embattled. The Lord said in the scriptures before He was taken back up to heaven that He had many rooms. He was going to this place, and He would come back and take us to that place. It was a home that had many rooms. Aretha Franklin went home yesterday to the room that Jesus had prepared for her. Her work on this earth was done. She now sings in the heavenly choir in a place that has been chosen just for her.

AUGUST 18

~Day 231~

Good Morning

Jesus is right now seating at the right hand of the Father. He is remembering and calling up our names before the Heavenly Father. I get goose bumps thinking about His great love for us. If you are experiencing some doubts this morning or evening, know that He is sharing all of your anxieties, problems, concerns, and issues. Right now, as I look out my window, the sky is overcast and cloudy. I can guarantee you that it will not stay that way for long. Sometimes, we have problems that seem to bring dark clouds and a black, overcast feel to our souls. Have no fear; the darkness will pass, and the true light will shine. We need to bring our cares, our burdens, and our sorrows to the only one who can truly heal them. Take your concerns to the one who has the answers and who knows the true way.

AUGUST 19

~Day 232~

Thankful

I am thankful that I had a mother who raised me to have healthy self-esteem. She raised me not to be in competition with anyone other than myself. She raised me to appreciate and love my skin, eyes, hair, and my inner beauty. By the time a person is eighteen years of age, they will hear between sixty thousand and a hundred thousand negative comments. Many of these negative comments coming from within our own families. I am thankful that my mom loved me and nourished my self-worth in a positive spirit and nature. Praise God and walk in thankfulness today. You were created in the image of God. You were wonderfully made in Christ.

AUGUST 20

~Day 233~

Keep the Faith

When we wonder if we will ever have a peaceful day of news, keep the faith. When we think that human relationships are hard to manage and navigate, keep the faith. When we wonder if we will ever experience true peace and friendship, keep the faith. When we want to express our displeasure and anger at an unjust situation, keep the faith. When we have experienced cruelty at the hands of a love one, keep the faith. When we are unsure of the next path or road that we must take, keep the faith. When we are doubting our belief in God, keep the faith. The Lord is either up ahead of us or just around the corner. He is always available to guide you to your greatest path. Keep the faith today. Walk in His anointing today by keeping the faith.

AUGUST 21

~Day 234~

Change

Don't fear change. Change is going to come to all of us during some point in our lives. We have to be open to the possibilities that things will not always stay the same. We need to be open to the realization that our routine patterns may not stay the same. Why do we fear change? We fear change because we might not be able to control events or situations around us. Don't fear change. Look upon change as an opportunity to grow in life. I used to fear change. I wanted everything to stay the same way. When we think in those terms, our children will never grow and start their own lives. If change does not happen, we will not grow our relationships with people and God. We should always be willing to change. Don't fear change but walk in the discovery of a new day.

AUGUST 22

~Day 235~

Transitions

Seasons change. Time changes. People change. Transitions happen in our lives. Transitions happen in life. Change happens, and we need to learn to welcome these periods of change in our lives. Some people hate for something different to happen in their work or play environments. We as humans get too comfortable with the sameness of everything in our lives. I know that I get too comfortable with my routine. I fight to keep routine in my day, and I also struggle to embrace transitions. True, there are all kinds of transitions in our lives. We have smooth, rocky, big, and small transitions. I am working on this area in my life. I need to do better with transitions. Don't get struck because you don't like change. Embrace the transitions of life. We only have one shot at it.

AUGUST 23

~Day 236~

Sounds

Hearing is truly a gift from God. When we have the ability to hear sounds, we learn a lot about our surroundings and people. The other day, I was talking on the telephone with a friend, and she did not sound well. I could hear sadness in her voice. I asked her if she was okay, if everything was going okay in her life. She shared some things that had been troubling her. I gave her some scripture that hopefully helped in the situation. Listen to the sounds of people, and be light and salt in a lonely and dark world. Be a good friend to someone today.

AUGUST 24

~Day 237~

Interesting

Look around you. I mean really look around you, and open your eyes to see the beauty of life. We take time and space for granted. Don't be impatient about taking the time to really look at people and value their presence in your life. People should not be a burden but an added plus to our lives. Look at how beautiful and wonderfully made we are as God's handiwork. We are all sisters and brothers made by the same Creator. How interesting! Isn't that interesting? Take a moment from your busy schedule today, and hit the pause button. Take a moment, and look around and see how interesting life can truly be.

AUGUST 25

~Day 238~

Massage

Hey, when was the last time you did something good for yourself? When was the last time you had a massage? I remember the first time I experienced the joy of my whole body being in a state of pure rest. No stress, no strain. Just pure peace and joy. We took a trip to the Bahamas to celebrate my sisters' fiftieth birthday. We had a blast. The water was the warmest water I have ever experienced. I stayed in the water the entire time. The massage that I experienced on the beach that day released stress that I had been carrying for years. When I got off the massage table and walked down the beach, I felt ten feet tall. I was free. I have learned that I need to release my burdens to my Heavenly Father. I occasionally get a massage to help lessen the stain and struggle in my neck. Question, when was the last time you had a great massage? Why not make an appointment to get rid of some of those heavy knots in your neck and back? Try it. You will see how much lighter your day can and will be.

AUGUST 26

~Day 239~

Sisters

I woke up this morning thinking about my sister who has been dead for thirty-one years today. She left this earth far too soon. My sister was a bright light within our family structure. She was very talented. She could dance, sing, sew, and knit. She had many friends, and people loved her. She was president of her senior class. She had a great math ability and was an excellent draftsperson. I wanted her to go to school for engineering, but she said not now. She was in love with life and with her husband and son. She had a great job and loved life. My soul aches to hear her laughter, her smile, and her great expressions regarding life. My sister would be happy to know that she has a beloved son who has the same smile as her. She would be happy to see the beautiful grandchildren that look exactly like her. She lives on in her son and grandchildren today. We are all blessed.

AUGUST 27

~Day 240~

Moments

Right at this moment, I am grateful to be alive. What is a moment in time? A moment is an indefinitely short period of time or value. Waking up this morning was an experience. It is important to enjoy moments in times. Don't take moments for granted. Life is short and moments are only instants in time. Moments are brief periods of time, but they have such impact on the direction of our lives. Don't take life for granted. Enjoy the moments in your life. Enjoy today and every day in the Lord!

AUGUST 28

~Day 241~

Farewells

I don't normally talk about a politician's farewell speech, but I was struck by John McCain's good-bye speech to the world. His last written remarks were deeply moving and powerful. He said something that really stuck with me: "Do not despair of our present difficulties, but believe always in the promise and greatness of America, because nothing is inevitable here." What a true statement, that "nothing is inevitable here." We need to live on this earth for today because we only have today. McCain's words are great reminders to us today as we walk this earth. The only one who is truly in control is God. We will take nothing with us when we leave this earth. We need to remember that we brought nothing with us when we entered this world. God is with us always. Do not despair. Farewells will happen. Things will come and go, but God is always on the throne. We are not to despair.

AUGUST 29

~Day 242~

Unhappiness

When you have no hope and you don't know Christ, you will feel a sense of hopelessness and despondency. You will have no joy in your life without the infilling of the Holy Spirit. I believe it is important to teach children early the stories in the scriptures. It is important for them to know Queen Esther, Mary, Martha, Daniel in the lions' den, and Jesus of Nazareth. Take some time and relearn those exciting stories of faith, truth, compassion, understanding, and deep love. We would have less unhappiness in the world if we took the truths of the scriptures and applied them in our lives daily.

AUGUST 30

~Day 243~

Soul Mates

When you find your soul mate, you will know it. I found my soul mate. I thank God for my soul mate. You want to know how you will know if that individual is your soul mate? That person is the last one in the hospital room when all other folks have left the room. Your soul mate is the person who will pick up something up from the store that you like, and you did not even have to ask them to get it for you. Your soul mate is the one who continually encourages you in whatever you do. Your soul mate is the individual who will gently evaluate your work or tell you when you are crazy for even thinking a certain thought. Your soul mate is the person, who says, "I got you" and truly mean it. Wait for your soul mate.

AUGUST 31

~Day 244~

God's Timing

How do we know to love the right person, at the right time? How do we know to trust the right person at the right time? How do we know in what city or town to live? How do we know what to invest in? How do we know what to say yes to and what to say no to at the right time? I believe with all my heart, mind, soul, body that we must trust in our Heavenly Father to guide and instruct us in all things. As the birds of the air and the animals in the field are under God's watchful care, so are we who love the Lord. It says in the New International Bible, "The Lord watches over all those who love Him." He watches over our entire existence, and He will take care of us, as He does, the woodpecker, the rabbit, the birds, and the bears. He will take care of you. Ask for His guidance today, and you will be under His timing for all things.

SEPTEMBER 1

~Day 245~

Choices

You can make a choice today to have a positive attitude about life. When you woke up this morning, you had that choice whether or not to be kind to people. You have the power to choose which way your day will go today. You have the option to be loving or cruel. Your choice. You have the mind-set and the control of this day. You only get this one day, but you have a choice. You have a choice on how you plan to interact with the human race today. So many people woke up this morning without having any ability or control of where they go and what they do. You do. Make your choices wisely today. Make your choices today with grace, mercy, and love. Choices are gifts from God.

SEPTEMBER 2

~Day 246~

Preparation and Guidelines

When I was a child, I brushed my teeth only when my mother told me. I did not want to brush my teeth every day because I was too busy with other things in life. I thought that the process of brushing my teeth was a waste of time. I had places to go and things to do. I viewed it as a waste of time and did not see brushing my teeth as a preparation for keeping all my teeth. I lost several of my teeth due to lack of care. I did not follow my mother's guidelines. What a waste! I should have listened and followed the guidelines. We do the same thing when we do not read the Bible and listen to God's word. We do not follow the process of reading, meditating, and allowing the Holy Spirit to instruct us. We don't follow the guidelines of the scriptures, and therefore we drift and we make mistakes. I wished that I could go back and do what my mother said, and maybe I would not have such costly implants. Read your word daily, and it will direct your paths in the ways that you should go.

SEPTEMBER 3

~Day 247~

Chill

I have always respected the significance of Labor Day. This day was hard fought for by the workers of America. It is fitting and proper to rest and chill today. To rest the body, mind, and soul. I have always honored the traditions of Labor Day. This day helps to restore body and soul. You need to hit the pause button sometimes and just chill. Chill in your body, chill in your mind, chill in your speech. As I look out of my window, I see just a little glimpse of fall coming around the corner. It is ninety degrees here, but I see some of the tree leaves slowly beginning to change. They are taking a moment to chill before they leave for their rest. You should chill today and restore your body, mind, and soul.

SEPTEMBER 4

~Day 248~

Unconditional

Jesus came on this earth, and He blew us away. He did not conform to the conditions, norms, or patterns of this world. He landed on this earth, and he loved everyone unconditionally. He tried to set an example for his disciples and for all the people he met on the roads of life. As we travel on life's highway today, we need to stretch ourselves in our love departments. We need to extend our borders of unconditional love in our hearts and walk in His examples of love. He loves you. He loves me. He loves us with our warts and all. Isn't that amazing? Walk in His love for you today because it is simply unconditional and affirming.

SEPTEMBER 5

~Day 249~

Take Some Time

I should have listened to an old saint's advice: "There are few things that can't wait twenty-four hours." He was right. Within that twenty-four hours, I could have taken the matter to God and had a more in-depth conversation with Him. Be wise today; take more time to seek His direction and wisdom. I plan to learn from my mistake and grow in my walk with God. Be smarter than me. Take everything to God in prayer. Sometimes, we move things along too fast. My nature is to move very quickly. The Lord has been teaching me to trust Him more and not my lean on my own reactions and nature. What about you?

SEPTEMBER 6

~Day 250~

Learning Some New

Teaching online is something that I always feared. I didn't want to post the wrong thing or hit the wrong key. I thought in my head that I didn't know enough about computers. It was a whole new territory for me. A new experience and a new venture. I said to myself, "Okay, this is something new; just move through it." The work took me a long time to complete. I worked for several hours and successfully completed the first assignment. I can do this. This morning, I am a little excited about this new adventure. I will learn and engage in this new way of teaching. A new way to learn and grow. Try something new today.

SEPTEMBER 7

~Day 251~

Difference

Today is a new day. Totally different from yesterday. Yesterday is truly gone and will not come back. You want to know something. Yesterday can't come back, and it is now set in history. You can make a difference with today. If you messed up something yesterday, you can make a difference with your today. Today is a gift to you from God. You can try and solve that problem with new eyes. The difference with today is that it is new, and you have it right now. Let go of the brokenness of yesterday. Walk in the newness and differences of this day. We have many challenges ahead of us this day, but we walk under the anointing of the Holy Spirit. Just let go of yesterday and journey into today knowing that you can make a difference.

SEPTEMBER 8

~Day 252~

My Mom

My mom would have been ninety-two years old today. Amazing. She did not live out her fiftieth birthday on this earth. I can only imagine the knowledge that she would have obtained by this time. I wished that I had the pleasure of knowing her as a ninety-year-old person. She would have been awesome. I knew my mom was special from the beginning. She always was different than other mothers. She worked outside the home. She had to work to feed five children. My mother loved us with unconditional love. She loved people, sports, and life, and she deeply loved her children. She always gave me excellent advice. Unfortunately, I did not always take her advice. I should have. It would have saved me a great deal of heartache. I grieve my mom today. She would have been ninety-two. Her children would have been fighting over whom she would have lived with as she aged. The funny thing about that situation is that she would have lived by herself. She was a very independent woman ahead of her time.

SEPTEMBER 9

~Day 253~

Fall

I woke up this morning, and it was cold. No heat. Fall is coming, and it is coming fast. When I awoke this morning, I could feel cold in my bones. Fall is coming fast. Fall has a purpose. It is a season of getting us ready for the coldness and the darkness of winter. Fall is preparation time. It is time to get ready for many things. The fall is upon us. We need to start preparing for a new winter and a new season. Fall is the time to generate all of this preparation. The squirrels and the rabbits are working away on their deadlines. We need to move forward with our plans and get ready for the exciting time of winter.

SEPTEMBER 10

~Day 254~

Calm

Today is a new day. Today is a day to stay calm or learn to be calm. How is your day going so far? Are you upset or are you at peace with yourself and everyone around you? Have you given thanks for today? Have you taken a moment to thank God for waking you up this morning? If not take a moment as you are reading this Daily Window. Hit the pause button. Okay. Is your body already stirred up in fifty thousand knots? Release them and let them go. Do not be a prisoner to any of your emotions today. Calm down and enjoy the day. Life is far too short. We don't seem to understand that life moves so quickly. We get caught up in senseless arguments and disagreements that linger far too long. Change your disposition today, and try to be calm. Calm down and enjoy the day.

SEPTEMBER 11

~Day 255~

Waiting Again

I am again back in the waiting room. Why do I spend so much time in the waiting room? What further lessons am I to learn? I thought I had gotten the message. I thought I had gotten a pass for a while. I guess not, because here I am again. I look around and I see a variety of people. Maybe I will learn something from one of them. As I wait to see the doctor, I decide to sit down to write this Daily Window. My name got called right away. Who would have thought? I am shocked. I go into the room, and the doctor takes me right away. It was a great visit, and I learned that I don't have to wait long sometimes. Good thought to process today.

SEPTEMBER 12

~Day 256~

Gym Ministry

I have a new ministry. I call it my gym ministry. I love it. I go to the gym several times a week, and I always meet new and exciting people. People love to talk, and they seem even more open to talk in the gym. As we get to know each other from the fitness classes, some folks will ask me what I do for work. When I say what I do for a career, they are excited to tell me their church story. I listen very quietly and then invite them to come with me to one of our weekly church services. No pressure. What a great new ministry. Think about looking for some new and exciting ministry opportunities.

SEPTEMBER 13

~Day 257~

Unexpected Interruptions

Unexpected interruptions that we face in life can sometimes bring unexpected opportunities. We can get so bent out of shape when our day does not go exactly the way we think that it should go. Sometimes, unexpected interruptions can change the course or projection of our lives. I remember that I was at work one day with a million things piled on my desk. My assistant came into my office and said that a man with a bicycle was walking around in our gym. I said to myself, "Why didn't she handle this interruption? I have a desk load of work to do and didn't need any further delays. I went into the gym, and I saw this man standing and looking around. Something in my head said, "Be kind and thoughtful." I know that the Holy Spirit was speaking quietly to me. The man introduced himself and said that he lived right around the corner. I would eventually get to know that home well. As we talked and shared during those few moments, my life was changed. This man during an unexpected interruption would become my lead professor in my doctoral program. What an unexpected opportunity! Don't view every unexpected interruption in your life as a nuisance.

SEPTEMBER 14

~Day 258~

Yelling

Yelling is something that I can't stomach. I grew up with people yelling all around me. The people in my building were always yelling and cussing. I associate yelling with anger. Why is it necessary to have a raised voice? I don't know. I leave the room when this craziness starts. I have no time for these inappropriate scenes in my life. Life is too short. Check yourself and ask yourself, "How am I speaking to my loved ones? How am I speaking to my coworkers and the people around me? Is my verbal message reflecting that I am a caring and concerned individual?" Check yourself. You never know you might not be communicating on a positive note. You wonder why some people might be avoiding you? Check out whether you are yelling today!

SEPTEMBER 15

~Day 259~

Here

So today we are here. We are present in this life. God has spared us one more moment in time. He has allowed us to cross over into another day and time. Are you in the here? Are you present in your life existence? Or are you just going through the motions of life? Are you just barely getting by on oxygen? My "here" changed for me when I met Jesus Christ. My whole presence of here and life changed in an instant. I became whole and I was born again. I was given a new *here*. Time is short. Life is short. I want my here, my life, my presence, and my existence to count on this earth. I want to leave a mark on this great planet. I want people to experience the *here* that I know in the living presence.

SEPTEMBER 16

~Day 260~

Words Matter

We live in a society today where everything seems to matter. Black lives matter. People matter. Green matters. Lives matter. Peace matters. Words matter. The words that we say to each other have life and action. You know what? Words matter. Words are action. I spoke to a wise friend about words and got this message: "Take what is truth from the words, and leave the rest at the door." I did just that. Words matter. Words matter. Actions matter. Think before you speak today, and remember that words matter.

SEPTEMBER 17

~Day 261~

Family Crisis

What is family to you? Family matters. Family is a unit of individuals who are together either through blood or united by love. We are family. Family is forged from time and essence of time. You were assigned to a family unit from the heavenly allotment center. Special delivery. Special packing. Handle with care. You were sent to continue this family unit. Family matters. You weather the storms of life together. Those storms can be major hurricanes or tornados. Family helps us to address major crises that can come against the unit. What kind of crisis are you dealing with today? Spiritual, personal, financial, or emotional—the family unit will be there for support and encouragement. We must be a unit of love in the midst of the dark rain that can come our way.

SEPTEMBER 18

~Day 262~

Friends

I went to early morning prayer this morning. It was great. We had a good time in prayer. I love the morning freshness of the day. The day is new and fresh. New opportunities. A new deck of life cards to draw. You learn a great deal when you pray with other people. There is a bonding experience that takes place that does not happen in other settings. Also, it is great when you share with a friend that you can trust. In the midst of the prayer times, I have found a great friend. A friend is someone who is someone who's got your back. I have great regard for this friend whom I talk to after our corporate prayer time. We hang out in the church parking lot and solve all the problems of the world. It is a great fellowship time. No masks are worn by either of us. Honest discussions about life and people are held in the parking lot. I don't like small talk. I probably would have advanced further in my career if I had been better at small talk. Small talk is not in my wheelhouse. I think small talk is a waste of time. I prefer deep conversations about with real friends. Friends are important. Seek to find a few good friends. You will not have many true friends in your lives. Value the people who speak truth and wisdom to you. These folks don't come along very often.

SEPTEMBER 19

~Day 263~

Service

We are not here just to serve ourselves; we have a greater purpose in life. We are here to serve our Heavenly Father. Think about it. What are you doing in service for the body? Are you sensing feelings of loneliness? Loss? Lack of companionship? You will find fellowship and joy in service with the body. Trust me. I know of what I speak. It is pure joy to serve in service for my Lord and Savior. I didn't think that I ever wanted to teach Sunday school again. How wrong I was. I love it. Teaching this class brings pure joy to my life. Think about a possibility of service in your life. What gift, talent, or skill can you give in service today?

SEPTEMBER 20

~Day 264~

Mind-Set

I would say to you today, just take it easy. Change your mind-set and don't allow your emotions to get control of your situation. Say to yourself, "We are not going there today." Sing a little song. Don't allow the darkness capture your thoughts. Rebuke it in the name of Jesus. Get the fleas off yourself. Get some space. Wave through the emotions and keep stepping. Hang in there. You are a survivor. Actually, you are more than a survivor; you are a pacesetter. Keep moving and looking forward. Get your mind-set in the right order. You may be blue today, but tomorrow is to be a brighter day. Tomorrow is going to be better. I know it. I sense it.

SEPTEMBER 21

~Day 265~

Confidence

You remember that I talked about your mind-set yesterday. Well, today, I want to address the area of confidence. Confidence is confident in oneself. I see far too many people walking the streets of life and not having any belief in themselves. This has got to change. Individuals need to rise up and walk in their anointed gifts. If you are feeling somewhat down today, get over it and walk like you have some sense. Life is too short. You have to be brave in this world and walk with your head high. You must walk today in an area of strength. Don't let the dark clouds of doubt overcast you and take your joy away today. Be brave. Be daring. Be bold. Be confident.

SEPTEMBER 22

~Day 266~

Disappointment

We have a choice to make. We have all seen people who wear their depression twenty-four seven. We can choose to wear the fragrance of disappointment or chose to wear a new fragrance called reappointment. To reappoint is to rearrange our time and energy into a different way or purpose, not to focus on what was lost. We can't pick up and reuse spilled milk. It is no longer any good. It is a disappointment because it was the only milk we had for the cereal. Okay—make some egg whites instead, and move on with your day. God can help us with all of our senses and emotions. He gave them to us. He can guide, instruct, and help us in whatever is going on in our lives. We need only to trust God in whatever situation we find ourselves.

SEPTEMBER 23

~Day 267~

Praise Him

What am I trying to say this morning in this Daily Window? I am saying to give praise to God. Give God the credit that is due Him. We take so many things for granted. Don't we? Before you start to complain about what you don't have today, expand your mind and give God the glory! Think about what He has done for you in the past. He was with you before the beginning of time. He was with you when you were in school. He was with you in all things. Praise God. He has allowed us on the journey. Praise Him!

SEPTEMBER 24

~Day 268~

You Can Do It

As I reflect from my cloudy window today, I am reminded of something that my mother told me. She said, "You can do it!" Those words stick in my head and heart today. I would ask her opinion on some job opportunity or some goal that I wanted to achieve. She was always in my corner and would say, "You can do it." When she said that to me, I believed that I could conquer any mountain or cross any river without a boat. She was in my corner. I want you to know today that you can do it. I am in your corner. Whatever goal or challenge you have in front of you today, know deep within your soul you can do it! Walk today in the confidence that you can do all things through Christ. He is walking ahead of you and guiding you in all things. You are a winner. You are more than a conqueror! God's got your back! You can do it! Just believe.

SEPTEMBER 25

~Day 269~

Every Day

Every day, we are going to have new challenges, new mountains, and new goals to achieve. Do not become discouraged or downhearted. Today is a new day. Every day is a new opportunity to make the goal of the day. Every day is a new chance to get it right today. Every day is a new deck of cards waiting to be dealt. Every day is a new opportunity to be in relationship with Jesus. Every day is a new opportunity to be in fellowship with the body of Christ. Every day is a new opportunity to meet new people. Every day is a new day to begin again. Every day is a new you. Walk in confidence that you are on the right track today because this is your every day.

SEPTEMBER 26

~Day 270~

Brush It Off

Brush off any negative thinking that might be trying to get in your way today. Rebuke it in the name of Jesus! Today, I went to meet my sister at the cemetery. This is the spot that is a mutual place for us to meet. The cemetery is the halfway point for both of us. We get an opportunity to say hello to my mother, father, and brother, and sometimes we go to the other cemetery to visit with my sister. We meet to conduct some family business. As I was waiting for my sister to come, my mind started looking at all the graves in the cemetery. I started to think some very dark thoughts. I said to myself, "Don't go down that memory lane. Don't go there. Brush it off. Don't spoil your mood or day." I am thankful for a God that loves us and is watching over us. Brush off any negative thoughts today.

SEPTEMBER 27

~Day 271~

Stay Strong

Good morning. This is the day that the Lord has made. We will rejoice and be glad. We need to thank God for His many, many mercies. The sun is trying to shine through the night clouds. We will rejoice and be glad to be part of this new day. We love you, Lord. Thank you for watching over us throughout the night. I want to tell you that no matter what you are going through today, stay strong. You are made from strong stock. If you are going through some type of challenge today, stay strong. You are loved with an everlasting love. Stay strong in your convictions.

SEPTEMBER 28

~Day 272~

Patience

It has always been said that patience is a virtue. We hear that word spoken a lot, but what does it really mean? Virtue means living a life with a moral code of ethics. Got it now. I think of patience in action. The action being when we need to think for a moment before we speak. When we become upset, we need to take a moment to bring our emotions into check. Patience is being careful with the way we talk to one another. Marriage helped me in the area of patience. Think before you speak. You cannot take words back. Words hurt. You can forgive but our minds do not allow us to forget. Go easy and be patient today, tomorrow, and definitely next week.

SEPTEMBER 29

~Day 273~

New

Today is a new day. It is occurring afresh at this very moment in time. We have been granted new moments and new opportunities for this fresh day. What are you going to do with it? Waste it on yesterday's problems? Yesterday's worries? Yesterday's mistakes? Not me. I am going to embrace this new fresh day with a new, fresh smile on my face. What are you going to do? Get into an argument with a friend. Make negative comments about life. Wear a frown on your face the size of Texas. Be smart. Be brave. Be grown up and embrace the day in newness of life. Full of joy and in the spirit of the Lord! Walk boldly into this new day.

SEPTEMBER 30

~Day 274~

Be Authentic

We cannot allow the politics of society keep us from having genuine and real conversations about subjects that are hard and difficult. We see in society so many walls, with divided friends. We are not supposed to sit in judgment about our friends because they disagree with our opinions. We need to be authentic in our faith about loving God with all of our heart, mind, soul, and being. And secondly, to love our neighbors as ourselves. If we do these two commandments, we can be authentic in our faith, in our love, and in our walk on this earth. We can be authentic about our relationships. Be real. Be genuine in your relationships today and every day.

OCTOBER 1

~Day 275~

Autumn Day

Don't waste your day with negative thoughts. Trust me, I know. Hear me. Don't waste your time with yesterday's worries and concerns. Yesterday is no longer here. We are in a new day. We have been allowed to cross over into a new day. Value this moment and time. Trust me, I know. I don't want to waste another moment worrying about something that I can't control in life. Stop it. Don't even go there! As I look out my window, I am so thankful to be able to see the beauty of autumn. I have to say honestly that as I look back on my journey, I should have looked at the trees more. I value life more now. Do I value life more now because I have less of it now? Or is it because I finally got it? We need to value life and the beauty of the moment now. When did I finally realize all that anxiety, stress, and worry did not change one thing? I am still learning. Look out your window, the window of life, and take in the beauty of the day. Trust me. I know.

OCTOBER 2

~Day 276~

Tuesdays

I love Tuesdays. Do you want to know why? I now start my day with early morning prayer at the church with other saints. It is a very powerful time in the Lord. You could say why go to church to pray? You can pray at home. I do pray at home, but it is always good to go and be in the fellowship with the body of Christ. In the Bible, it talks about not giving up the habit of meeting together as a group of believers. I believe there will come a time when we will not be allowed to meet together to pray. I want to enjoy this season of grace. When I leave the group after our prayer time, I feel in my spirit that I could climb a mountain. The presence of the Lord is always there. I walk under that anointing today. Find a church group that is healthy, and join the praying team. You will feel blessed, and you will be blessed.

OCTOBER 3

~Day 277~

Rejoice

Good morning. I wanted to say to you today, "Rejoice!" Do you know what rejoice means? It means to feel and express joy in life. Do you feel glad today? If you do not, I would like to remind you of a few things. You did not have a tsunami come to your house yesterday and take it away. You did not have a hurricane last night or a flooded house or basement today. You had dinner last night and did not have to search for water in the desert. Are you rejoicing yet? Not sure? Rejoice and be glad that you are free to say what you want to say, go where you want to go, and buy what you want to buy. I just finished reading a book of fiction that only allowed women in society to speak one hundred words a day. Can you imagine only being allowed to speak a few words a day? You can say anything you want right now. Rejoice and thank God for the day!

OCTOBER 4

~Day 278~

Thursday

This is a special day. It is Thursday. I guess it is also like a Sabbath rest day for me. I use to have to work on Sundays. I always appreciated the rest in my soul on Thursdays. Love you greatly. Enjoy this Thursday. What day of the week gives you more joy? Think about it. I pray that you have a favorite day. I love all the days of the week, but I guess I just love Thursdays. Maybe there is some hidden memory in my soul that I have been unable to reclaim. Maybe one day it will come to me. We will see and share. What about you? Think great thoughts today.

OCTOBER 5

~Day 279~

Wisdom

I ask God for wisdom and discernment because it makes my life go smoother. Wisdom helps me to grow and learn. Wisdom give me joy in the midst of the darkness. Wisdom eases the pain that I feel inside of my soul and bones. Wisdom can right my day and enrich my night. Wisdom in thought and deed helps to keep me out of darkness and trouble. Wisdom calms the seas and engages the light. Wisdom helps to fill my days with joy and sunshine. Wisdom helps to stop the dark clouds that try to come when a storm approaches our lives. God's wisdom is the best wisdom in the universe. Seek and you shall find. Knock and the door will be open to you. What is true or right coupled with just judgment and with action thrown in for spice and favor? If you are wondering about something, ask God to give you wisdom.

OCTOBER 6

~Day 280~

Off

Do you ever sometimes start your day "off"? I mean, when everything is moving differently than you? You are going at a different pace than the rest of the world or the individuals around you. I have experienced this "off" all day long. I am a little frustrated about every little thing that is going on. What's up with that? When that happens to you, I want to give you some good advice. Get in a quiet space and chill. You might need to reboot. Your body is telling you to slow down for a minute. When you feel "off," you need to take a break from everything and everyone. Just chill down for an hour or so. Trust me, I know. You will be a better human being in an hour or so.

OCTOBER 7

~Day 281~

Just Sharing

I have had a love of the scriptures for a long, long time. I remember when I was thirteen years old; every day after school I would come home and read the Bible. I did not always understand everything I read. I would read for a long time struggling with my King James Version. I did not have a good grasp of the word, but I knew that God was calling me. I just didn't know what that meant. I did not understand what a calling was and what to do with it. Just sharing. As I grew older, I found my truth in the word of God. Just sharing. I have always known that I was meant to preach the word of God. Don't ask me how I knew—I just knew.

OCTOBER 8

~Day 282~

Checking In

How are you doing? I am just checking in on you. It is important to do a check in on occasion. How are you feeling? Are you okay? Are you happy? What I really mean is, are you fulfilled in life? Do you have joy? Are you experiencing joy in life? I pray so. I want to tell you a secret. Life is short. Life gets shorter every day. I was praying with a woman at the altar yesterday, and she shared several things with me. She said that I had prayed with her several years ago and that the prayers had been helpful. At that time, we anointed her and she felt at peace. She was just checking in with me. We need to check in with one another. How is your soul today? I pray that it is in excellent condition.

OCTOBER 9

~Day 283~

Online Courses

I'm not sure if I would recommend taking an online course with your spouse early in your marriage. I learned a number of things about my spouse by taking this course with him. Initially, I thought it would be a great idea for us to do this together. I thought it would be great bonding time. Really? Today, I am unsure. The jury is still out. I will let you know when the six weeks are finished. The concept of working together in the beginning was very romantic. It sounded like a great idea, but we both work differently. I love to finish my deadlines ten days before the due date. My spouse likes to finish on the day that the project is due. Not a good combination. We will walk by faith and not sight in this process. Online may become offline. Have a great day in the Lord.

OCTOBER 10

~Day 284~

Hang in There

If you are tired today, hang in there. If you are worried about something, hang in there. If you are upset about something, hang in there. If you are concerned about bills, hang in there. If you don't like your job today, hang in there. If your family and friends are not responsive to you today, hang in there. Whatever state of mind that you happen to find yourself in today, hang in there. I know without a shadow of a doubt that God is on His throne and that He cares about us. I know without a shadow of a doubt that His angels are watching over us. I pray with all my heart that you believe that God will see you through any fears, doubts, conditions, emotions, or tiredness. Hang in there. Hope and peace are right around the bend.

OCTOBER 11

~Day 285~

Reunions

I attended my fiftieth high school reunion. Amazing. How far and how old I have become. I am excited. I don't feel old. I actually feel better than I did twenty-five years ago. I remember going to my twenty-fifth anniversary, and there were only seven women who attended the celebration.

When I graduated from high school, things were very difficult. We had just passed the voter registration rights bill, and people were testing the law all over the country. Racial tension was everywhere. People were suspicious of everything and everyone. Kind of like now. We were all isolated in school. I now believe we all struggled with PTSD. The entire class of 1968 had problems. I looked up the disorder, and my class definitely showed signs of all the symptoms of it: I believe Post traumatic stress disorder is an anxiety disorder that affects many people in life and it affected me and my fellow classmates. I can see it clearly now many of my friends might have had this disorder. How all that stress affected our minds and bodies. I am thankful that God came into my life and set me free.

OCTOBER 12

~Day 286~

Reunion Memories

Where did time go? Where did those fifty years go? I am searching my mind. Where did time go? I just turned around, and I was seventeen years old. I was a kid growing up fast in a city. We lived in the midst of a hurricane of life's issues continuing to sweep over us. I was a kid worrying about things that I should never have to worry about. We lived in fear. We lived with shots being fired throughout the night. Riots were happening all around the city. Boston was a hotbed of anger and violence. Both Martin Luther King and Robert Kennedy were killed within two months of each other. No one knew what to do with their fears and disappointments. They took their rage out on others. Where did the time go? I would not have made it without the saving grace of Jesus Christ. To God be the glory!

OCTOBER 13

~Day 287~

Laughter

I am sitting at my desk looking out the window of life and thanking God for His goodness. I am thankful for God's promises and His love for me and you. I am laughing because I have joy deep down in my soul. My prayer for you today is to become more flexible and enjoy life to the fullest. Do you know that laughter is good for the soul? You want to know why? Laughter helps you ease up on yourself. You should not take yourself so seriously in life! If we take a moment to laugh at ourselves, we can get ourselves into a chill-down state. If you don't laugh at yourself sometimes, you will take yourself far too seriously.

OCTOBER 14

~Day 288~

Excited

I am excited about life. I am excited that I can read, drive, and walk. I went to the registry the other day to renew my license. I had to wait two hours. I am truly excited that I passed the test with flying colors. I saw a man ahead of me who looked about seventy-five years of age. He had to take the eye test twice. I do not want to be on the road with him. I gave him a double look over. I am excited that I finished my online course. I am so excited. I survived it. I actually think I am one of the top students in the class. I am excited! I pray that you are excited about something today in Jesus. Walk in excitement today and every day.

OCTOBER 15

~Day 289~

Big Fun

I had a great time at the reunion. I had big fun. I was the greeter for the reunion. I believe one 160 women came through the doors of the event. I must have received at least 160 compliments. Wow! Big fun! It was great to be with the people. I love being involved in ministry work that advances the kingdom of God. Think about the things that cause you to have big fun and do them today. Do something positive today and have big fun.

OCTOBER 16

~Day 290~

Your Vote

If you don't vote, don't complain. I heard a statistic that has caused me to really ponder. One of my students stated that fifteen million people did not vote in the past national election. How could that happen? Some people did not take the time to vote. These same people who did not vote are now complaining about what is happening in society. My question is why? They should have expressed their true opinion at the voting booth. I have had my say in the matter. I voted. Did you? We believe in a democracy. I shared my views and expressed my opinion. I rest my case until another opportunity to change the vote again. What about you?

OCTOBER 17

~Day 291~

Results

I believe the town election results are in, but I don't know what was decided. Typically, we hear the results the very next day. Not the case today. You want to know what? It doesn't really matter that I don't know the final results yet. You want to know why I say that? It is because what truly matters is that I voted yesterday. I stood up. I was counted in the number. I matter. My vote matters. My little vote counted for something. I just don't know what that something is just at the moment. We will see in due time. My vote mattered and I am a part of this community. I exercised my right to vote yesterday. Did you?

OCTOBER 18

~Day 292~

Random

This is a very random message today. Hang in there. Some days just seem to slip away, and you just have to go with the randomness of it. I love God. I love life. I love my husband. I love my family. I love you who read this Daily Window. Hang in there. The day has gone quickly. Hang in there. Where does time go? Hang in there.

OCTOBER 19

~Day 293~

Alone

Satan is a liar. He tries to put negative thoughts in our heads. You know what you have to do: rebuke Satan in the name of Jesus! That's right—rebuke him in the mighty name of Jesus. Jesus is the only one who can sustain us and give us eternal life. Praise God. In the scriptures, one of the last things Jesus said on earth is, "I will be with you and I will never forsake you." I carry those words in my heart daily. The words are living and real. Trust me, I know of which I speak. Try them on for size, and I am sure that they will fit. You are never alone. God has your back.

OCTOBER 20

~Day 294~

Talk

I have seen in my lifetime far too many people who fail to reach out and talk with one another. We need to really hear what is being said and really talk about what we are hearing to have full understanding. Talk with one another and listen. Talk. It is important to talk with one another. Talking is communicate or exchange ideas by speaking. We are people who were created to communicate with one another. If we don't talk properly to one another, walls could be created. Walls are difficult to tear down. We must talk with one another on a continual basis.

OCTOBER 21

~Day 295~

Calling

Do you know what a calling is? A calling is a strong pull or inclination to do something. It is something that you feel that you must do. You don't have peace in your soul unless you do this assignment. This is the way that I felt when I got the call to preach and teach. It was that way when I felt the need to go to school. What is your calling? Have you found it yet? Trust me, it is calling to you. You will know your calling when you sense it totally in your spirit, body, and soul. God has a calling for everyone who trusts and obey.

OCTOBER 22

~Day 296~

Increase

My definition today of increase is more of something good. I want to increase in my wisdom levels. I want to increase what I have learned on this earth. I want to increase in learning new things. I am so excited about the new things that I have learned from my online course. I have increased my knowledge base. I love teaching. I love increasing my knowledge regarding teaching. I pray that you increase in your wisdom, increase in your happiness, and definitely increase in your joy levels. The only thing that I do not want an increase in at this time is snow. What would you like to increase in today?

OCTOBER 23

~Day 297~

Release

It is important to release any ill feelings you have toward things, people, and stuff. What happens to us when we carry around all these extra loads of things? I can tell you: a great deal of hardships, emotions, and sometimes physical pains. No one else is carrying the junk around, but you are still thinking about the comments of 2011 made about you. Forget it. Release it. If you are carrying something today, release it and move on with your life.

OCTOBER 24

~Day 298~

Today

We only have today. "Today" means this "present time." This present age. We only have these moments. I am enjoying this day. I look outside my window, and I see the beauty of God's nature. The trees and their beautiful colors of fall. Only God can create these awesome colors. Look around you as you walk through the day. Look above you as you experience the sky above. We only have today. Don't sleepwalk through your day. Stop. Look around you and embrace your surroundings. Take a moment to thank God for allowing you to be a part of such an awesome day in time. Enjoy and be glad. This day will never come again. Take the time to be present in this great moment of life. Be present in this moment.

OCTOBER 25

~Day 299~

Seasons

I look out my window, and I see the beauty of the fall. The colors are so beautiful. I am really loving nature this year. I wonder why? I believe it is because I never took the time before to be present in the moment. I was always behind or moving too fast by looking ahead to quickly. I have missed many present moments. At times, I have to calm myself down and say to myself, *Enjoy this time in your life. You have worked hard with the help of the Holy Spirit to get to this moment. Chill and slow down. Enjoy the seasons of this moment.*

These seasons are awesome to behold. I am truly enjoying the seasons now. Christmas is two months from today. I truly can't wait to be present in those moments.

OCTOBER 26

~Day 300~

Be Smart

Be smart with your words that you think and words that you share. Be smart with the thoughts that you have in your head. Be smart with the thoughts that are in your heart. What I mean by being smart is this: don't allow someone else's emotions or issues to affect your soul. Be smart in how you allow individuals to drain your energy. Be smart and don't allow others to bring you down when you are feeling great. You need to be smart and enjoy these moments of life.

OCTOBER 27

~Day 301~

Stay the Course

When you are in the middle of a battle and the storm is raging. You must stay the course. You must stay the course in the direction that God has given for your life. Don't allow anyone or anything to put you down. People would like for you to think negatively about yourself. You matter. You must stay the course and be strong in your resolve to please God. Don't allow ugly moments to define your destiny. You have to be strong and not allow the words of others to impact your day and life. I was reading over the life of Christ, and people said some pretty mean things to Him. Jesus stayed the course that He needed to go for you and me. Stay the course. Be calm. Be smart. Be focused.

OCTOBER 28

~Day 302~

Visiting

I love to visit churches. I love to visit churches that I have attended in the past. Visiting is going to or staying with (a person or family) or at (a place) for a short time for reasons of fellowship or business opportunities. I love going to visit for a short period of time. I went to a church today that I had not visited in eight years. We had a wonderful time of fellowship. It was great to see the people, and they were excited to see me. It was a memorable experience that I will think of fondly in the future. I believe the members of the church will also think of our time together as memorable. Visiting can be a wonderful thing. Enjoy your times in fellowship with other saints.

OCTOBER 29

~Day 303~

New Monday

Hey, do you know what? Today is a new day. A new start. A new Monday. You know what? Last Monday is gone, and it is never coming back to us. It is done. Was it a good or bad Monday? Do you even remember? Last Monday is in our rearview mirrors. Basically, what I am saying is that yesterday is in the sea of forgetfulness. You have to move on and embrace the new Monday. You have to make room in your mind, heart, and soul for the new Monday. If we embrace this newness of thinking, we will be better human beings. I am serious. You will like and love yourself better if you just let go of some of the old garbage. I use to carry around with me a whole bunch of nasty Mondays. When I let go of those Mondays, it was like taking a gorilla off my head and shoulders. I was free. Don't you want to be free today? Enjoy your Monday and embrace this new day.

OCTOBER 30

~Day 304~

Trains

I love trains. I love the way trains look. I love the way they feel. I love the movement of the train. I believe there is a calmness to the ride. Every time I take a train, I sense more peace than on a plane or in a car. I love watching people on the train. There are so many different types of people riding in the same directions but all going separate places. The train is like a little United Nations all of its own. So many different varieties of human beings collected in one place. Amazing grace. Amazing movement of life. Enjoy a train ride soon, and experience some peace and tranquility in your life.

OCTOBER 31

~Day 305~

Fear

This is the last day of October, and it was a beautiful autumn day. A piece of advice: Don't allow fear to keep you from your true destiny. The first step is to really trust in God. Trust in God and listen to His voice. You will never go wrong. With a sincere heart and mind, you put your faith and trust in God. I have walked down many unsure paths, and I knew that God was always me. I learned to listen to Him. The second step is not to be afraid. Remember, you are not walking down the path by yourself. God is leading you in the direction that you should go. Trust God with everything. Be faithful to His word and actions. With a sincere heart, don't make your decisions in fear. It's okay to be unsure, but don't allow fear to wrap chains around your heart and mind. Walk by faith and not by sight.

NOVEMBER 1

~Day 306~

Daily Bread

Give us this day our daily bread. You remember that prayer line? In this prayer God tells us to ask for our daily bread. He gives us enough for today. Sometimes, we expand our minds and try to focus on things too far down the road. He gives us our daily bread today. We don't own tomorrow. Don't be afraid. Don't be anxious or stressed. We can sometimes get ourselves in trouble for focusing too far down the road. The Lord says in His word that He takes care of the needs of the birds in the air; how much more will He provide for you and me? We have to trust God to provide our daily bread. We have to stop worrying about tomorrow's needs.

NOVEMBER 2

~Day 307~

Celebrate

Today is a day to celebrate. Do you have something to celebrate today? Wait a minute. Think about it for a few seconds. Of course, you have something to celebrate. You know what? You are alive. You woke up this morning. Your stomach is not empty. You had a meal in the past twenty-four hours. Your house has some heat. You have clean air to breathe. You have people who love you. You have people who happen to like you and respect you. You have family who will help you and assist you in a crisis. You have been loved. Celebrate that you are not alone in the world. You have a God who is bigger than you are in life. Celebrate both little and big things in life. Celebrate the gift of life that God has given to you today! Walk under the umbrella of God's anointing on your life. Celebrate His goodness to you.

NOVEMBER 3

~Day 308~

Listening

If you want to communicate well with others, you have to have the ability to listen closely to the message that is coming to your ears and minds. We have to be open to receive new data and not just rely on old information. Recently, I attended a meeting where no one in the room wanted to learn any new information. Every board member kept going back to the old way of doing things. It is important to be mindful to listen and learn something new every day. To listen means, to really give attention to the words expressed by another human being. Let us be open to listening to one another in love and peace. We all need to listen and grow.

NOVEMBER 4

~Day 309~

Fifty-Eight

The number fifty-eight means different things to different people. Fifty-eight could be the number of times you had a piece of pie or chocolate cake. Fifty-eight could represent the degrees to which the temperature is outside of your window. Fifty-eight could mean the score that you receive on a test. Today, fifty-eight represents the number of years that my youngest sister has existed on this earth. Today is her birthday. I remember the day she was born just like it was yesterday. I thought that this was the day that my mother was going to die. My mother was nine months pregnant, and we were extremely poor. We had little heat and no food in our apartment. We also did not have a telephone to call anyone for help. My father was at work. Winter was in full gear, and heavy snow was on the ground. We must have had at least two feet of snow. My mother was in severe pain and kicked us out of the living room. She had my sister on the floor. Such a dark, lonely, and cold floor. I ran to a neighbor's house to get the police to come. God was with my mom and family. His grace is sufficient in all things. Walk in His grace today.

NOVEMBER 5

~Day 310~

Patience

I am frustrated by a bunch of little things today. I don't want those "little foxes" to get in the way of stealing my joy. I need to take charge and control of my inner spirit and practice patience. Patience requires practice. You have to control your emotions and not allow your emotions to control you. You don't want your lack of patience to direct your path for the day. I want to remember the goodness of God and enjoy my day. I have shaken off my "fleas of impatience," and now have a better control of my day and my journey in Christ. Walk under the direction and guidance of the Holy Spirit, and then we can produce the fruit of the spirit. Have more patience today on your journey!

NOVEMBER 6

~Day 311~

Differences

We are made in all different shapes, styles, and sizes. We are different. We have many differences. You want to know what? It is okay for us to have our differences. You want to know why? We have each been uniquely made by God. It is important to be your own identity. To be your own personhood. I was talking with someone today, and they said that they had lost their identity to someone else. What a shame. In the beginning, they stated that they were okay, but they slowly lost themselves. She is slowly finding her new self. Walk in your destiny and your special life. You are special and uniquely made in the eyes of the Lord. You are very special. Walk in that specialness. You are different. Work in your living differences and uniqueness.

NOVEMBER 7

~Day 312~

Vacations

We are going on vacation. I am excited about going away to rest on a beautiful tropical island. I love hearing the sound of the ocean and seeing the different and beautiful trees. Vacations are a time to relax from any form of labor. I am looking forward to a period of suspension and just sitting on the beach with my Kindle. Think about going on a period of suspension from work, things, issues, and crises. Learn to rest your mind, body, and soul. I plan to have a great time in the Lord! I look forward to eating some great food and reading some great books. I have downloaded at least twenty new books. I am excited. Join me. Have a great day in the Lord! Blessings today and every day. Think about taking a vacation soon.

NOVEMBER 8

~Day 313~

Vacation Tired

I almost forgot what I was supposed to do today. I have been so involved in my vacation ventures that I almost forgot to post my Daily Window. How could that almost happen? I got caught up in vacation tiredness. I have been too busy with trying to take part in everything that my eyes see. Don't get me wrong; I enjoyed everything that I did today, but I think I got a bit overinvolved. I need to slow my roll down just a bit. I also need to try to get a bit more sleep. When you are away from home, your daily routine gets broken. Oh, how I like routine. I am definitely a creature of habit. But you know what? It is sometimes good to break our patterns. I am going to get over my vacation tiredness by going to bed and getting some needed rest. What about you?

NOVEMBER 9

~Day 314~

The Beach

I look around my environment today, and I am just so thankful for this time. I look around and I am sitting on the beach in eighty-degree weather and feeling great. I know that where I came from, it is raining cats and dogs. It is also extremely cold. I am sitting on the beach, and the sun is still shining bright! I look at the people on the beach, and I see people from everywhere and from every culture. I love it! The people are interesting to watch. Enjoy your experience today. Basically, enjoy life and be calm. Be cool. Be focused.

NOVEMBER 10

~Day 315~

Forgot

I forgot something. I knew that I had forgotten something in my mind. I forgot to do my Daily Window. How did that happen? I am so diligent about doing the Daily Window. When something like this happens, the only thing that you can do is give yourself grace. When you have forgotten something and it was not intentional, you have to allow yourself some slack. You cannot beat up yourself and ruin your day! You have to move on in the grace that God has given you. I plan to move on with my day and time! You should move on with your day if you have forgotten to do something. Forgive yourself.

NOVEMBER 11

~Day 316~

Say Hello

What is happening to society today? I think I know. We all think we know. I believe that we need Jesus Christ in our hearts and minds and souls and bodies. Walk today in the anointing of the Holy Spirit, and say hello to a fellow traveler that you meet on the road of life. My mother taught me many lessons. At the time I did not know that they were lessons of life. One of the lessons that she taught me was that you were to give everyone you see the grace of day. What do I mean by "the grace of day"? It's to say hello, speak to people, look them in their eyes, and acknowledge their existence. This lesson that my mother taught me is both a powerful one and insightful one. Say hello to someone today, and give them the grace of day.

NOVEMBER 12

~Day 317~

Aruba

In all the months that I have been writing the Daily Window, I have never spoken about Aruba. I found my second home. I was sharing with someone the other day that the moment I got off the plane in Aruba, I felt a state of peace. I let my guard down, and my whole body just went into a place of rest. I've been to a number of places before but never felt such peace. Aruba is called "the Happy Island." I can see why. The water is beautiful, the sky is blue, the sun is shining, and the trade winds are always flowing. I pray that you have a place of peace to call your second home.

NOVEMBER 13

~Day 318~

My Dad

Today is my father's birthday, and he would have been ninety-four years old. He died when he was sixty-eight years of age. He died eleven days before his sixty-ninth birthday. He did not make it to his seventieth birthday. My father loved his family in his own way. I knew that he was proud of our accomplishments as a family. The people that I met on his job knew everything about our schooling, our awards, and our promotions. I will see Dad again because before he died, he accepted Christ as his Savior. I know that my mother and father have reconciled their differences. I know they always loved each other. I believe the love of Christ helped them reach a new level of understanding. Walk in the anointing of the Lord today, and have peace with everyone!

NOVEMBER 14

~Day 319~

The Happy Island

I can understand why Aruba is called the Happy Island. The majority of the economy here is based on tourism. The residents of Aruba understand what it takes to retain repeat customers. Everyone I talk to on the beach are repeat customers, and they happen to love the island. I love that you can look out your window and see the ocean. I love the fact that you can go right down to the gym and find all the towels, machines, and assistance available to you. I love the fact that you can go to a number of restaurants and have quality food and quality service. I love the fact that the majority of the people on the beach are friendly. There are some folks who look at you as though you have four heads. That's okay. You're going to find a few bad apples in any bunch. Each day brings a new opportunity to have a complete and restful experience. Aruba helps to refresh my soul as we travel in a dry and desolate place. Enjoy life! Enjoy piece! Enjoy the journey!

NOVEMBER 15

~Day 320~

Special Time

I am still in Aruba and having a great time. This is a special time because I am more aware than ever that time is shorter than the day before. Time passes quickly but moves slowly, so it seems. I am having a great time learning about family, responsibilities, jobs, and life. I am becoming who I was meant to be. I was meant to be a person who is full of love, a wife to a wonderful husband, a mother to two beautiful daughters, and a mother-in-love to my children's husbands. I am becoming the person that I was supposed to be, and I'm thankful that God has given me an opportunity to see things through the lens of the Holy Spirit. If you have any doubt or confusion about anything, check out the word of God, and your confusion will definitely go away.

NOVEMBER 16

~Day 321~

Late Post

My late post message to you today is rest, look around up in the sky, and thank God that you are able to read. One of the ladies that I've met here in Aruba has been losing her sight. I am thankful and grateful for the gift of sight and the ability to be able to read. Enjoy life and don't worry so much. Praise God. Take your time today, and just rest in the Lord.

NOVEMBER 17

~Day 322~

Hut Line

One of the things that I really like about Aruba is that I get an opportunity to observe and meet new people every day. One of my daily routines is to get a new hut on the beach each day. You have to go a couple of hours early to get into the hut line. I have had the opportunity to meet some of the most interesting people in the world. Everyone comes to have conversation and get to know new people. I have been in the line with some of the same people for the past several years. It is interesting to talk to them about their children, and I talk about my children as if we are old friends. It is an interesting social dynamic. One of my joys that I will always treasure in life is to meet new people. Enjoy your day, smile, and start your own hut line.

NOVEMBER 18

~Day 323~

My Last Beach Day

This is my last beach day in Aruba. I am little sad, but I am rested and ready to go and deal with the snow back in New England. This is the first time we are going back to snow in November. We have been here almost two weeks, and we have had a really great time. I always feel blessed that I have discovered my second home, Aruba. As I've shared in past Daily Windows, I consider Aruba a second home. It is a place that has always seem to embrace me, and I just fell in love with the culture, the people, the water, and the peace of the beach. I am already looking forward to my next adventure here on the island. Look for your next adventure in the spirit of the Lord.

NOVEMBER 19

~Day 324~

Leaving I Will Be

This country of Aruba has entered into my very soul. When something enters your soul, it captures your heart. I pray I keep this love for a long time. I leave the country of Aruba feeling very rested and refreshed and rejuvenated in my soul. The land does that "something" to me. The water of the Aruban ocean rejuvenates me and gives me renewed strength. I leave today not brokenhearted but full of joy and love. I walk in joy and renewed strength and with the Savior who claims my soul. I pray that you find your spot of pure joy, hope, and peace.

NOVEMBER 20

~Day 325~

Home

I am home. We have been away for almost two weeks and have had a great time. However, there is nothing like coming home. There are many definitions of the word *home*. The one that I would select for my emotions today is "a dwelling place or sacred space." I sense that sacredness in my home. I have space to breathe and to grow. I have space in my home to think, not think, or just to be me. I loved my vacation, but I also love my home. When I entered through the door last night, I said within my heart and mind that it was great to be here. My soul sang a new song. I said aloud to the house, "Did you miss us?" I believe that a house takes on the "norms and emotions" of the people who stay with the walls of the house—not haunted or anything, just some specialness about your space. I believe our homes have been happy homes. It was great to be home. As I look out my window today, it is raining and there is no sunshine, but it is sunny in my home today. Are you at peace in your home?

NOVEMBER 21

~Day 326~

It's My Birthday

Today is my birthday. I am so grateful that I have my health and strength. I am grateful that God has guided me and instructed me in all things. I am grateful that I have a family who cares about me and loves me for my own special personhood. I am grateful to be alive. My mother lived to be barely fifty years of age. The last five years of her life was spent living in pain with cancer. My father did not see his sixty-ninth birthday. I pray that my genes from ancient relatives will be stronger and more sustainable. Where did time go? I am so grateful for the memories. Oh, what a day! What a special journey this is, and I continue to marvel in its richness. What special memories do you have today? Not sure? Go out and create new ones.

NOVEMBER 22

~Day 327~

Thanksgiving

As I look out my window and get ready to travel for this season, my pearl of wisdom for you today is to be generous with your spirit of kindness. Be generous with your patience today. Be generous with holding your tongue. Don't say it; you might regret the comments tomorrow and realize that you truly hurt the person by those misspoken words. Be generous in your love of family, friends, and acquaintances today. You only get this one day. Trust me, I know that time passes quickly, but it seems to move slowly. Trust me. Time is moving rapidly. Don't mess up today with any negative or smelly thoughts. Love life and love the people around you. Be generous with your love, patience, and respect of human life.

NOVEMBER 23

~Day 328~

Cold

No matter how cold it is, I am thankful for this day. I'm thankful for the opportunity to be able to walk and talk and to have the reason of my own mind. I am thankful and grateful for memories. I am thankful to be able to feel the cold and be a part of life's journey. I am thankful for my family and for all the new memories that we will make today. I am thankful for the Holy Spirit being in my life and guiding me in all things. I would like to suggest to you to seek the Holy Spirit and His guidance in all things. What are you thankful for today? What are you searching for today? He can help you.

NOVEMBER 24

~Day 329~

Resolved

I woke up this morning with the word "resolved" on my mind. What I mean by resolved is to deal with or solve a problem. I woke up pretty focused today and wanted to get started on my day. I have let some things go unfinished or not get started on time. I need to get moving and get my brain in gear. I need to get focused on my daily priorities and move forward. I need to get back to my daily routines. I am resolved to get focused and get my act together. I want to resolve a few things in my brain that I have been carrying around in the head cart of my mind. Resolved. I am resolved to address my checklist today. I need to get some items checked off my list. I have to pick up the pieces of my mind and get working on moving forward. I need to get my act together tomorrow. What about you? Are you resolved with your many lists today?

NOVEMBER 25

~Day 330~

The Lord's Day

I can remember growing up, and my mother would say that Sundays was the Lord's Day. What she meant by that was that we should honor God with our time and with our obedience. We had to be quieter in the house on Sundays. Sunday was the Lord's Day. We were to spend some time of our day honoring the King of Kings and giving thanks for all that He had done for us in the past week. We could not go to the store nor shop. We had to be respectful of the day. We could not be loud. I have since expanded my own interpretation of the Lord's Day. The Lord's Day is every day. We are supposed to honor and glorify Him in all that we do. We are to set aside some part of each day and give Him thanks. It was He who made us, and it was He who woke us up this morning. God has always loved us even before our beings came into existence. He gave us life. The Lord's Day is truly every day. He gave us this day, and we need not waste it. We need to honor Him with our love, respect, and worship. He has given us everything. It is only right to give back to Him a portion of all that He has given us. Remember today is the Lord's Day. Remember that every day is the Lord's Day. Walk under His anointing power.

NOVEMBER 26

~Day 331~

Share

One of the most important things that we can do as human beings is to share. We were created to be in community with others, and in that process, we need to share of ourselves with others. We all have gifts that were given to us by our Heavenly Father. The Holy Spirit imparted each person with at least one gift. The gift is to be shared with the body of Christ. I see so many people isolated and lonely. I see so many people not using the gifts that God has given them to use in this wonderful world. You must share your gifts with others, and you will be truly blessed in this life. I would suggest that you discover what your gift is and use that special gift. Share it with the people around you. Be generous today with your gift and your love.

NOVEMBER 27

~Day 332~

Searching

Are you searching for something today? To search means to look for or discover something that might be missing. Are you searching for something today? I am always looking for new discoveries. Today, I cleaned out my linen closet. I have not cleaned out that closet in years. I was afraid of what I would find when I started to dig down deep. I was searching to get rid of old towels and stuff. In the process, I discovered some new towels and stuff that I had not utilized in a long time. What a discovery! I had put this task off for such a long time, and in the middle of the pile was some truly great stuff. Are you searching for something today? Are you looking to discover new things? New opportunities? Don't be afraid to dive into new adventures and new opportunities. I took too long to tackle the linen closet. Walk in the anointing that has been placed on your life. Do not be afraid to search and discover new opportunities of growth and learning.

NOVEMBER 28

~Day 333~

Stay in Faith

I will remain in fellowship and love with my Heavenly Father, no matter what the storms of life. I have had my share of doubts, pains, and sorrow, but my trust and faith are in God. I try to do my spiritual disciplines daily, and they definitely help to strengthen my walk and faith in Christ. If I was to give you some advice today, I would say to stay in faith and not waver in your belief. Read your Bible. Read the book of Ephesians, and then head on over to 2 Corinthians to see what the apostle Paul went through in his life. He stayed the course and was found faithful. Stay the course and stay in faith. The way we stay in faith is by turning all our doubts, fears, anxieties over to *Him*. He will help and guide us all. Stay in faith.

NOVEMBER 29

~Day 334~

Walk in Faith

Yesterday's Daily Window was talking about staying in faith. Staying means to "stay put" right where you are in your faith. I think that is a good way to be in life. I also think that we must walk daily in faith. We cannot stay or live in a bubble. We have to get out into the public square every day and face the challenges that life throws at us. We must walk by faith and not by sight. Every day is not going to be perfect; people are not always going to treat us well. We were not created to able to see everything that is going to happen around us. We must walk by faith in Jesus Christ. We are to walk in faith, believing that God is in control of the universe. We are to put our trust in the Holy One of Israel. Walk in faith this day believing that you are going to be and do well!

NOVEMBER 30

~Day 335~

Last Day

This is the last day. The last day of November. This day will never come again. You know what? You need to take a moment and just stop. Pause. I think about all the things that could have gone wrong this month, but they did not. I think about all the things that I worried about, and they did not happen. I think about all the things that I was anxious about, and they did not happen. I think about all the protection that God has given each of us. We walk under the anointing of God's protection. Even when we are hurt and wounded, we are still under the protection of our Heavenly Father. This is the last day of November; please take a moment and shout praise unto our Lord and Savior. Walk in His grace this day and every day.

DECEMBER 1

~Day 336~

Mood Swings

Each day is different, and we must embrace the newness of each day. Every day is not going to be perfect. We have to make room for differences. We will have things in life that will be drainers and not much fun. I don't think shopping for groceries is a lot of fun when my mood swings in a negative way. On other days I love shopping and picking up new items to try. When I was younger, I stayed in a negative mood swing and ruined everyone's day. Not now. I have too much life to live. I have too much live to give. I am going to make the most of my day. What about you? We will not get this day again. What about you and your mood swings? Rejoice and be glad. Change your mood with joy if your mood is swinging negative.

DECEMBER 2

~Day 337~

Timing

I believe that the best timing in life is God's timing. In the scriptures, God tells us that there is a season for everything under the sun. I think that just about covers everything. It is not wisdom to get yourself into a despairing state of mind. It is important to have faith that everything is going to work out fine in God's timing. We like to hurry things, just like Christmas—shopping too early and rushing the sacred moments of life. It is good to wait in expectancy of the goodness of the Advent season. We have a lot to learn along the way as we wait for the coming of the King. Take a pause today, and allow God's timing in all things and everything under the sun.

DECEMBER 3

~Day 338~

Keep Trusting

Today is a new day. It is a new day with new adventures, opportunities, trials, and potential disappointments. My word of encouragement to you today is to keep trusting in the faith that you received by the Holy Spirit. God deposited His Spirit in your heart and soul. Keep trusting in that deposit. Keep trusting in the God who created you. Unfortunately, many of the people you come in contact with today do not know the Lord. They do not know that they can trust in a God who controls all the universes. So, people rely on their own trust and skills. Not good. They create problems for themselves and everyone else. Trust me, I know. You must keep trusting in God, even in the dark days. I can remember growing up in the projects, and I would say to myself, "Lord, is it ever going to get better?" I kept praying. I kept trusting in God. I have to admit, I was shaky at times, but I believed God would see me through my trials and tribulations. It took twenty-five years to get out of that bondage and craziness. God was with me the whole time. Keep trusting. He will set you free.

DECEMBER 4

~Day 339~

Blessed

Every day I feel blessed. Do you? There are many definitions and meanings for the word "blessed." Today, I am kind of moved and motivated by "divinely or supremely favored." I count myself to be very favored and fortunate for everything that I have in my life. I am truly blessed. I woke up in a home that does not belong to the bank or anyone trying to take it away from us. I woke up this morning with heat in my home. I woke up this morning having the ability to see with my own eyes and have the capability to read with understanding. I am feeling blessed this morning because no one had to help me get out of bed. What do you feel blessed about today?

DECEMBER 5

~Day 340~

Continual Blessings

I thank God for His continual blessings. He doesn't have to do it, but He does. God loves us. God continually loves us continually. I went to class last night, and I thought that I had everything that I needed to conduct my class. I started to lecture and looked in my briefcase, and I saw that I didn't have my textbook. Can you believe that? I have never gone to class without my textbook. I panicked for two seconds and said to the students that I would not be able to ask them all the questions that I had prepared. I informed them that I had forgotten my book. I think I saw some of them actually smile. However, by God's continual blessings, I had some great lecture notes. Praise God that I had those notes. The notes saved my lecture and added quality class time. God's continual blessings. God saved me again last night. Receive God's continual blessings in your life today. Don't panic. Trust that God will see you through the craziness of life's busy streets.

DECEMBER 6

~Day 341~

Upset

I am upset by the way society treats our elderly citizens. I was in a doctor's office recently, and I observed this poor woman having to wait for over an hour and a half for service. The request that she had was only a minor thing regarding her eyeglasses. The sales representative said that she would have to wait. I observed the elderly lady going over and standing by the door for the man to see her. Perhaps he had forgotten that she was there? She was waiting a long, long time. It can happen, but that was not the case in this situation. The elderly lady must have been close to ninety years of age. She fell asleep for a few minutes due to the long wait time. The elderly lady was still sitting in the chair when I left. I thought about speaking to the man. We need to treat all peoples well, especially our elderly. What would Jesus do?

DECEMBER 7

~Day 342~

Let Me Process That

I have learned over time to take the processing time to take everything to God in prayer, in dealing with both big and small things in life. I have learned some harsh lessons along the way. It is better to ferment my concerns, life issues, and problems with my Heavenly Father. I know that the Holy Spirit guides and instructs us in life's concerns. I have a calmness that comes over me and quiets my spirit. I know when God has affirmed my prayers. It does take time and practice to hear His still, calm, and quiet voice. I am not racing when God responds to my prayer requests. I also know when God has said no to my requests; I sometimes get a little frustrated. I have to be truthful—I am a little put down when I don't hear when I think I should hear. I am growing in this area. Trust God and process everything with Him.

DECEMBER 8

~Day 343~

Remain in Faith

Did God forget us? Do our prayers matter? First, God did not forget us. God does not forget anything or anyone. Our God is a big God. Yes, the scriptures tell us that our prayers matter. Why did God not answer those personal prayers that we have locked deep down in our souls? What is my responsibility in the middle of waiting for an answer? What am I supposed to do with myself? Doesn't God know I need an answer now? What's the problem with my request? You know what I must do? Do you know what you must do? We must remain in faith believing that God has everything covered. Jesus asked a question before He was taken from this earth: "Will the Son of Man find faith when He returns?" I want to be found faithful. How about you? Don't be so impatient. A thousand years is like a day to our Lord and Savior. Walk and remain in faith today and every day.

DECEMBER 9

~Day 344~

Sabbath Rest

Today is the Lord's Day. I use to hear my mother say that phrase when I was a young child. We could not do a lot of things on Sunday. We had to be quiet, and we could not run around outside like we normally did do the week. We could not shop and go to the grocery store. We could not hang out on the corner. We could not go to any regular stores, and the drugstores all closed at noon on Sunday. No banks were open to give you money. Society had to slow down on Sundays back in the day. I miss the quietness of the day. Sabbath is any special day of prayer or rest. Sabbath rest is a special time to rest the body, mind, and soul. Do you take a Sabbath rest? When was the last time? Take one today.

DECEMBER 10

~Day 345~

Special Events

Life is special. Did you know that? Life is a special event. Your life is special. Your birth was special. You are special. God created you uniquely to be you. On this earth, there will never be another person like you. Someone may copy your style or your looks, but they are only a carbon copy of the original. You are special. You are an original being. Made special in the heavenly oven. God applied the right favors and copyrighted your special blend. God created each one of us uniquely in His spirit and His essence. We need to live our lives in His directions and ways. God is the chairman of the ways and means committee of our lives. We do not live in isolation of thoughts and places. We have been brought with a price. We have each been brought by the birth and resurrection of our Lord and Savior. I feel so blessed that God created you and that you are truly a special event. I thank God that we were all created and that we are all special events for our Heavenly Father. Think on this thought today.

DECEMBER 11

~Day 346~

Encourager

The Bible talks a great deal about encouraging others. To encourage means to inspire with courage and give confidence in something to someone. It is important to encourage others to be and do their best that they can in this life. It is important to encourage others to fulfill the dreams that they have deep down baking in their souls. The apostle Paul encouraged people to grow and learn. He encouraged and inspired the young leaders of yesterday to walk by faith and not by sight. As I look around the world today, people in the world need to be encouraged. People need to be encouraged to do the right things and to say the right things. Be an encourager to someone today and every day.

DECEMBER 12

~Day 347~

New Patterns

You do not have to stay stuck in the way you do things in life. You can change or modify the way things happen in your life. I know because I have made many changes in my life. I praise God for being with me and challenging me to grow in *Him*. When I was a little child, we were dirt poor. We could not purchase toys for Christmas until Christmas Eve. We would run around to Woolworth's and try to pick up toys for my younger brother and sisters. We would place the toys under the tree just before they woke up on Christmas morning. We would find a tree that no one else wanted and drag it home to decorate. We typically ran out of heating oil, and it was a wonder that we didn't all die from cold or pneumonia. I decided that I would create new habits and patterns in my own home. I try to plan ahead the gifts and treats that I would like to give my loved ones. I chose to create new patterns or rhythms of life. Break free from whatever chains, habits, fears, and issues keep you from becoming your best self. Break free and create some new patterns today.

DECEMBER 13

~Day 348~

Make a Difference

Make a difference. Do you want to know how to make a difference today? You can make a difference in someone's life today. You can change the course of history and impact someone's life today. You want to know how you can make a difference today? You can speak a word of kindness to someone you don't even know in life. Better still, you can speak a word of kindness to someone you know in your family or extended group of friends. You know someone who is going through something today. The truth of the matter is that there is always someone going through something. We all need encouragement.

Make a difference in someone's life today. Encourage someone. If you are the person reading this and needing encouragement today, know that you are special. Know that you have a God who loves you unconditionally, and know that you have been prayed for by someone you don't even know. You will get through this fork in the road. The light is just ahead of you. Stay strong and stay faithful. Make a difference and change the course of history. Speak a word of kindness into someone's life today.

DECEMBER 14

~Day 349~

My View

As I have looked out my window of life today, I have begun to view "my view" through the lens of having a big God who knows the rest of the story. I use to say, "How is this ever going to happen or change? Am I ever going to get that job? Am I ever going to be a success at this project? As I ever going to be happy in this new place?" I had more questions than answers. I have learned a new view. I have learned that I have a big God. I believe I have a big God, and my faith is in *Him*. God has the big view. I have learned that my view is His view for my life. How did that happen?

I went to the Source. I took all of my worries, pains, burdens, and both negative and positive thoughts to Him. He gave me my answers. He led me in the correct path of life. I trust God. The most immediate task is to turn every need, every request, every thought, and every decision over to Him. He knows the path, the timing, and the view. Trust Him and He will give you the right view.

DECEMBER 15

~Day 350~

Short and Sweet

I would highly recommend to you today to read the book of James. The book is short. The messages that come from the Lord's brother James are awesome. Great for the soul. Short and sweet. The book only has five chapters and a lifetime of advice, wisdom, and help. The fifth chapter says, "Are you suffering hardships? You should pray. Are any of you happy? You should sing praises. Are any of you sick? You should call for the elders of the church to come and pray over you."

Short and sweet. Just like this devotional today. Short and sweet.

DECEMBER 16

~Day 351~

Frustrations

Trust me. You are going to get frustrated by things in life. What does it mean to be frustrated? It means, a feeling of dissatisfaction with something or someone and the matter stays unresolved. Trust me. We all get frustrated by things in this world. All you have to do is look around, and you could become frustrated by something or someone. As I look out my window this morning, I want to share with you not to allow your frustrations to rob you of your joy of this day. I have seen people be so frustrated by life's events, and they take their frustrations out on themselves by worrying, developing harmful habits, and having bad attitudes. Don't allow the frustrations of yesterday keep you from the joy of today and the living of tomorrow. So many people walk on this earth with the scars of frustration on them like a perfume. Be a person who is going to walk on this earth with a signature perfume that sends a signal or message of joy. Trust me. When something frustrates you today in word or deed, don't wear it as your perfume of the day. Walk in the anointing of the Living Savior, Jesus Christ.

DECEMBER 17

~Day 352~

Don't Quit

Yesterday, I talked about the things that can potentially frustrate us. As you go through your daily life, don't quit because you become frustrated with a situation. To quit something means that you stop something in midstream. There is a difference between stopping something at just the right time. There are some natural, progressive ways of leaving things in life. To leave a job or relationship, you have to really pray and seek the counsel of your Heavenly Father. There are jobs that we need to leave, but leave in the right way and spirit. I was talking with someone the other day about their Bible reading. The young woman told me that she quit her study in July. She shared that she had become depressed and had gotten away from the word. She just quit. I wished that she would have shared that statement with others. We could have helped her overcome her thoughts and assisted in helping her to press on. Instead of seeking help, she just quit. She was very disappointed in herself for dropping out of the program. She said that she became frustrated by so many things in life. We will have difficult seasons in life. We can't just quit on the journey of life. We must equip ourselves with the right tools to weather the storms of life. The clothing to wear today is the armor of God. Check it out—what is the armor of God? Pick up the word of God, and live in its presence.

DECEMBER 18

~Day 353~

Don't Waste Time

I have seen people waste their time on past hurts, and they can't move on in life. The emotional scars of life have worn them down, and they can't get up. These individuals continue to move in circles and never can seem to get up out of their own personal pits or holes. I have seen people waste their time on career goals that were not for them. These individuals blame everyone for their own shortcomings or mistakes that they have made. I have seen people spend far too much time thinking about the success that they thought they should have now, and they have not enjoyed the current moment. Don't waste your time with "should've, could've, or would've"; move on in the spirit of celebration of life, in its fullness, and enjoy today without shame, fear, or doubt. Don't waste time today!

DECEMBER 19

~Day 354~

Take a Break

As I look out my window, I feel blessed in the Lord. I am going to take a break and rest for the remainder of the day. I have to say that I had a rough night last night and did not sleep a second. I was sick. I have a hard time processing some medicines. I am grateful to be alive and feeling better today. Everyone needs to take a break every once in a while. Enjoy your day and take a break in your mind, body, heart, and soul. More serious Daily Windowing tomorrow.

DECEMBER 20

~Day 355~

Don't Worry

We worry about too many things in life. We torment ourselves over far too many things in life. We fret about everything and nothing. I would fret about a lot of things. I worried about work. You name it, I worried. I was the queen of worry. Finally, one day the Lord said to me, "Make a choice. Believe in me and trust me." I needed to step up and step into a faith relationship with God. I needed to believe that God would do what He does best in His own timing. I needed to not worry about the things of this world. I needed to let go and allow God to move fully in my life. Today, whatever you might be fretting or worrying over, turn it over to God. Trust me, I know of what I speak. I use to have the title of Queen Worrier. My title today is that I put everything into God's hands and trust Him in His timing. Don't worry. Allow God to do His thing.

DECEMBER 21

~Day 356~

The Longest Night

I can remember when my children were very small and I was working and going to school. I have to be honest and say that I really hated the winter months because the days were so short and it was so dark outside. I felt a darkness within me. I was so tired from all of the responsibilities of being a wife, mother, coworker, and student—not even counting the titles of sister, aunt, or friend on the list. I just felt a deep burden because each day became so dark so quickly.

At that time, I thought that I didn't have enough time to do all the things that I needed to accomplish in a day. I struggled with these thoughts for several years until a wise, godly woman shared something profound with me. She truly helped me change my outlook on the winter months and life in general. She shared with me that December 21 is the shortest day of the year and the longest night. I said to myself, "How is that going to help me?" Each day after December 22 adds a minute of sunlight. You do not know what that statement did to my mental attitude. It was as if I had a new lease on life and a new approach to the winter months. I love today. I know that this is the first official day of winter, but I know tomorrow is a brighter day. Seek out counsel from some wise, godly people and they will give you some godly advice.

DECEMBER 22

~Day 357~

Make a Call

As a society, we spend too much time texting and not having enough personal contact. Gone are the days that we just visited over at each other's homes. People used to travel and visit with family and friends for weeks at a time. I remember a cousin who visited us. She stayed for several weeks when I was a young child. When we talk directly to someone, we share a part of ourselves with that individual. We also send a message that we care and that we have taken the time to connect. Make a call. Cheer someone up. Go visit. Let them know that you care and that they are loved. You are loved today.

DECEMBER 23

~Day 358~

Memory Lane

As we head toward Christmas day, I always seem to take a trip down memory lane. Even as a young child, I use to think about the old days leading up to Christmas. I would think that the snow back in the day was the most beautiful snow that ever fell, and that we had fifty feet of it outside of our windows. I think about the food that we used to eat and how delicious and special the dishes were. We did not have much fruit or candy, as we do now. The stores back in the day only had certain fruits at certain times of the year. Now, you are able to get any type of fruit or food on demand. I think about the mistakes that I have made in life and ponder whether I could have done better. As I have gotten older, I think in a more simplistic manner now. Thank God. I see things without a whole lot of confusion. Is that a little bit of wisdom? I pray so. I have prayed for wisdom and guidance all of my life. I think about my family, and I feel a sense of being blessed by the Heavenly Father. I think of the struggles that my mother and father had when I was growing up. I feel blessed that we made it through all of the ups and downs. I am grateful for memory lane because I know that I am indeed a blessed child of the King. What are your memories? Good? Bad? Make new ones today!

DECEMBER 24

~Day 359~

Christmas Eve

Today is Christmas Eve. Amazing grace. God has spared us each for one more year of coming into His presence at this time. Christmas Eve is a time of family, friends, and faith renewed in the loving grace of Jesus Christ. We received the greatest gift that ever was created in our Lord and Savior. I am so grateful to my Heavenly Father for taking the time with me and giving me the gift of eternal life. Love your family and friends today. It's Christmas Eve. If you don't have a family to love today, then love a friend. If you don't have a friend to love, then make a new friend. There are over seven billion people in the world, and I know you can find and make some new friends.

DECEMBER 25

~Day 360~

Christmas Day

Today is Christmas Day. The most special day of the year. The coming of the King. We have been watching, waiting, and expecting this special day. This is the day that is going to change the existence of mankind. We are thankful for everything that God has provided for us. What a special day in the Lord! New memories are being made today. We started this special day with prayer and thanked God for everything in life. We created some new memories of love. You are awesome, Lord. This is His birthday, and we celebrate His birth every day. Awesome! Enjoy this season with love, joy, peace, hope, and always eternal love. Give the gift of love to someone who does not have love in their life. We need the light of our eternal Source forever. Give the gift of thanksgiving to someone today and the joy of Christmas spirit.

DECEMBER 26

~Day 361~

The Day after Christmas Day

This is the day after Christmas. Some people are running back to the stores to return unwanted or unneeded gifts. Some people are sad or lonely because all the events of Christmas are over. Some people feel blessed as I do because we created new memories in the spirit of joy. I am grateful for life and the fact that I have a Savior who loves me and listens to me. I have a Savior today who understands me and encourages me and guides me along a better path of life. What are you grateful for today? I pray that we grow more in the fruit of the spirit this year and the next year and the next year. Walk today in His anointing love, peace, and hope.

DECEMBER 27

~Day 362~

The Day after the Day after Christmas Day

Some folks are beginning to bring out their boxes to pack up their ornaments to be saved and used for next year. Some folks are packing up their trees or putting them in the garbage to be picked up on trash day. I like to ponder life the day after the day after Christmas Day. Do you want to know what I ponder about on this special day—the day after the day after Christmas Day? I ponder life itself. I do an early life assessment of what has happened around me. I think about the goodness of God and how grateful I am that He has allowed me the ability to see. I think about the goodness of God and am grateful for allowing me the skill of walking up and down stairs by myself. I ponder and thank God for the sense of hearing and the understanding of words and meanings. Take a moment as you look out your window, and look up toward the heavens and thank Him for providing this moment in time. You are blessed this day with memories. What do you ponder today?

DECEMBER 28

~Day 363~

Who's in Charge?

Who's in charge? Who's in charge of your life? It all starts with us submitting to His will and His way. It is about believing that God knows the way we should travel in this journey called life. God cares so much about us that He sent His only Son to reconcile us to Him. He did not have to do it. God wanted us to be in fellowship with us. We were created to be in fellowship with God. The beauty of the entire system is that God gives us a choice every day. We get to choose which way we will go; we get to choose who's in charge. We get to choose whether we want to follow His path. What an amazing God that we get a choice to say, "Who's in charge?" Who's in charge in your life today? I pray that you walk in the wisdom of the Heavenly Father. I made my choice, and I am living in the peace of Jesus Christ. What about you?

DECEMBER 29

~Day 364~

Alone

Do you remember the movie *Home Alone*, where the family went on vacation and they accidently left the youngest child at home? He goes through a series of adventures in the house, and he is not alone physically. His mother is shown crying and worrying that he is helpless and alone. In reality, he was having an adventure of a lifetime. I believe the movie industry made several different versions of the *Home Alone* story line. In real life, we are never "alone." You may say, "I was alone when this happened" or "My family or friends were not with me when I had that tragedy. One could also say, "No one was with me when I went to this place or that particular country."

I am talking today about something far deeper than a physical sense. I am speaking regarding a deeper inner sense of mind, body, and soul. When we allow Jesus Christ to have complete control of our hearts, mind, and souls, He resides within us. He is with us twenty-four seven. Amazing love. Amazing God. We have a choice. We made a choice every day. Do we want to go it alone and be on our own? Or will we allow the King of Kings to order our steps in this life? As I look through the window of life, I am extremely thankful and grateful that God whispers in my ear and tells me the path to take. I sometimes still get goose bumps just thinking about the times He has gotten my attention, and I am deeply touched in my inner core, my essence, and deep down in my soul. What about you?

DECEMBER 30

~Day 365~

Don't Forget

As I look out my window this early Sunday morning, the sky is overcast and gray. I am filled with joy because I know that my Savior lives and that He never forgets about me. He has been with me through every storm in my life, and I know that He will be with me in the end. I have no fear of tomorrow. I know that my Redeemer lives and that He will return one day and claim His children. The noises of society want to drown out the miracles of Christmas and the words from the Holy Scriptures. No way. The best advice of wisdom that I can give you today is don't forget He who stands at your right side. Don't forget who loves you unconditionally. Don't forget who died on the cross for you when you didn't even know Him. Don't forget that you are loved today and every day.

DECEMBER 31

~Day 366~

Moving Forward

Today is the last day of the year! Today is a day of celebration. You have almost made it through another year. Stop, shout, and praise the Lord right now! Think about all that you have accomplished in the past 365 days. Think about all that you have come through in this past year. Think about the good, the bad, and the ugly. I would suggest, looking out my window, that we should not live in the land of regrets. You need to remember today that God has brought you through everything in life. The good and the not-so-good things in life this year. As we move forward into the next year, please don't carry the negative thoughts, the despairing ideas, or burdens of this year. God has given us each a second chance to cross over into the newness of a new year. It is a great gift, and we should not waste this precious gift of life on past mistakes or the wrong path. Happy New Year, and blessings in moving forward today!

Made in the USA
Middletown, DE
15 December 2019